NEW YORK SCENE

Written and Compiled by

GERARD RAYMOND

THE GAY MEN'S PRESS

A special thank you, first to William Schwalbe and Ben Pesner without whom this book would not have been possible. My thanks also to David Klotz, for reading the manuscript, and all my other friends — including Dan Ebalo, Frank Headley, Mark Heidron, Mark Shenton (in London), Leslie Smith and Jeff Stockwell — who, like true New Yorkers, are experts in one field or another.

As far as possible, all information, including prices quoted in this book is accurate as of 1st June 1996.
Unless otherwise noted, all telephone numbers listed are in the Manhattan (212) area code.

First published 1996 by GMP Publishers Ltd,
PO Box 247, Swaffham, PE37 8PA, England

Stephen DiMenna would like to thank Sean Tierney, Joe Belmonte,
Michael Santo, Guy Colter Talent, and John Phillips Photoagraphy.

A CIP catalogue record for this book
is available from the British Library

ISBN 0 85449 228 3

Distributed in Europe by Central Books,
99 Wallis Road, London E9 5LN

Distributed in North America by InBook/LPC Group,
1436 West Randolph Street, Chicago, IL 60607

Distributed in Australia by Bulldog Books
PO Box 300, Beaconsfield, NSW 2014

Printed and bound in the EU by The Cromwell Press,
Melksham, Wilts, England

CONTENTS

WIGSTOCK Photo copyright © Tina Paul

1: INTRODUCTION

Welcome to New York — to all those magical names and places you know from books and the movies. It's a city of dreams. And nightmares, too. New York has the best of everything, including the best of the worst, wrote satirist H.L. Mencken. The center of high finance, culture and fashion, New York is stimulating, dazzling and sexy. It's also overcrowded, dirty and sometimes scary. But there is no place like New York.

No book can capture the variety, the idiosyncrasies and the unique joys of this multi-faceted metropolis. *New York Scene* concentrates on places of interest to gay men, not because it means in any way to be exclusionary, but because lesbian New York warrants a separate book altogether. This book gives you guidelines, tips and insider information that will help you feel like a New Yorker. Like you, many of the city's 7.3 million residents have come from elsewhere. Being a New Yorker isn't about race, nationality nor ethnicity; it's a matter of energy and personality.

Remember the three sailors in *On the Town* who had one day to see all of New York? I've lived here for twelve years, and still haven't done the city entirely. Don't try to fit it all on a single trip. Focus on what appeals to you most: Broadway theater, the Metropolitan Opera, drag shows, the avant-garde, the tacky, the ritzy, whatever — it's all here.

First, to dispel a myth: The natives are friendly. Ask for help or directions and you are more than likely to find New Yorkers obliging. Don't be put off by our brusque exteriors. Things move at a fast pace in this city and New Yorkers always seem to be rushing with little time for pleasantries. Our speech is often very direct; we will ask you who you are and where you come from in a straightforward way that may be considered bad manners somewhere else. We love to show off our city, and bitch about it as well. Everyone has an opinion and will express it loudly, from the garrulous taxi-driver to the aspiring actor/dancer/opera singer who is your waiter for the evening.

How dangerous is New York? No more so than anywhere else, if you keep your wits about you and don't flash your wallet. No, we do not all carry guns, and yes, you can walk on the streets after dark (within reason).

Is New York a gay city? You bet it is! It's one of the sexiest and most gay-friendly cities in the world. It's the Oz every Friend of Dorothy dreams of. We are everywhere. On the streets, in the subways, in restaurants or in the theaters, you'll catch that lingering look, the frank stare or just that cute smile which reveals how gay New York can be.

And, of course, New York has been very much a part of gay history and politics. The Stonewall uprising, the defining moment of the modern gay and lesbian liberation movement, took place in New York's Greenwich Village. To celebrate that event, hundreds of thousands of lesbians and gays march down Fifth Avenue every year. A lavender stripe is painted down the middle of the city's most famous avenue, and the Empire State Building, New York's most prominent landmark, is lit up lavender to mark the occasion. New York has also been in the vanguard fighting against AIDS. Both Gay Men's Health Crisis (GMHC) and the AIDS Coalition to Unleash Power (ACT UP), were founded in this city.

So here we are — New York, New York. You have arrived in the city that never sleeps, a bustling 24-hour metropolis. Some people live here for years and never feel part of it. But you may experience the rush of high energy that drives the city the moment you arrive and instantly feel at home. New York could be the greatest experience of your life, and your greatest challenge. But, as the song says, if you can make it here, you can make it anywhere. So once again, welcome to New York. Make it your city!

March 1994

1996 UPDATE

In the two years since *New York Scene* was first published New York City has seen many changes — some for the better (a greater police presence, cleaner and safer streets, more visitor-friendly services) and some for worse (a greater police presence, a Republican Mayor). But one thing has not changed. Every day of the year a new visitor comes to the Big Apple and re-discovers the uniqueness of this city. Now it's your turn.

May 1996

2: TRAVEL INFORMATION & GETTING AROUND

When New Yorkers say "the city", they usually mean Manhattan. There are four other boroughs in New York City — Brooklyn, Queens, the Bronx and Staten Island, but you will find that practically every famous place you've heard of in New York is located in the densely populated, 2.3 mile (3.7 km) wide, 13.4 mile (21.5 km) long island of Manhattan.

IMMIGRATION AND CUSTOMS

Gay visitors coming into New York usually don't encounter discrimination. Generally, if you have a valid passport, you should have no problems. Be prepared to show you can support yourself financially during your visit, and have a return ticket back home. Keep your feather boa discreetly packed in your suitcase until you clear immigration!

Your travel agent and airline will provide information regarding your duty-free allocations and what you can and cannot bring into America. You may carry pornography or sex toys as long as they are obviously for your own personal use and not for resale in the States. Discretion in these matters is advised, of course.

VISITORS WITH HIV/AIDS

Legally speaking, if you have HIV you must apply for and obtain a waiver of excludability (which could take 30 days or longer) along with your visa in order to enter the U.S. You must go through this process even if you're from a country that participates in the Visa Waiver Pilot Program which, ordinarily, entitles you to enter the country without a visa. Of course, most tourists simply opt not to disclose their HIV status, which simplifies matters. If you do not have visible signs of AIDS and are not carrying AIDS-specific medication or AIDS-related literature in your baggage, you'll probably avoid detection. Gay Men's Health Crisis (see Chapter 7) can help you obtain your medications locally.

AIRPORTS

Three major airports serve the city. Two of them, **John F. Kennedy International Airport** and **La Guardia Airport** are located in Queens, while **Newark International Airport** is in the neighboring state of New Jersey. If you are travelling alone, you'll find it most economical to travel into the city from all three airports by bus. Alas, there are no direct rail links to the airports. There are complicated bus-to-subway connections but they are not recommended if you are new to the city.

NOTE: The airports and bus terminals are the prime playgrounds for New York con artists. Laden with baggage and looking for the quickest way to get to your hotel, you're an easy target. Don't let anyone take your bags or offer to get you a taxi. **Be suspicious first!**

Follow the signs and take directions only from the official, uniformed taxi despatchers who are on duty at all three airports during peak hours. During off-peak hours uniformed Port Authority police officers and uniformed terminal security guards will assist you. Take only the taxis which operate from designated taxi stands at the various airports.

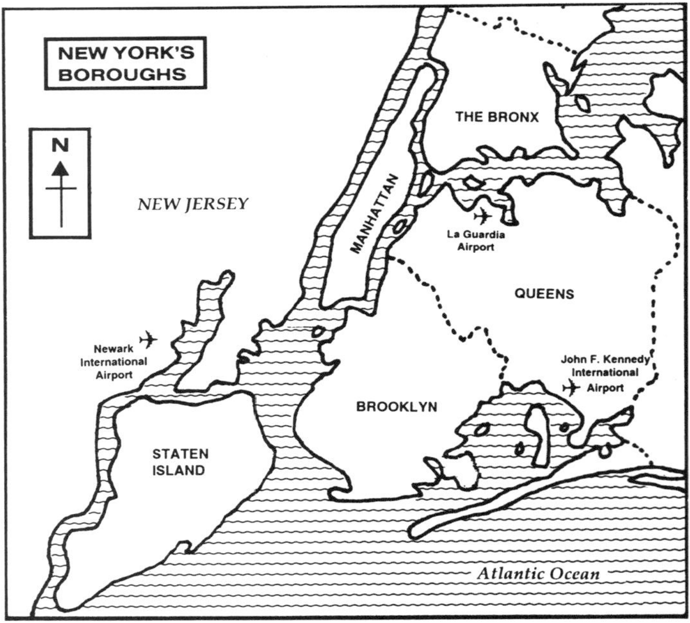

JOHN F. KENNEDY INTERNATIONAL

JFK is the busiest airport, located 15 miles from Manhattan (one hour's drive in traffic). Avoid flying via JFK if you can. You don't need the irritation of waiting in long lines for immigration (if you're coming from overseas) or for picking up your baggage.

Bus: Carey Transport express bus service. One-way rides cost $13 and may last over an hour depending on traffic and on how long it takes to sell tickets to all the passengers. The Carey bus makes two stops in Manhattan, at Grand Central Station

(Park Avenue between 41st and 42nd Streets), and the Port Authority Bus Terminal (42nd Street and 8th Avenue). For an extra $1.50 the bus takes you to the following hotels: the New York Hilton (53rd Street at Avenue of the Americas), Sheraton Manhattan (Seventh Avenue between 51st and 52nd Streets), Holiday Inn Crowne Plaza (48th Street at Broadway), and Marriott Marquis (Broadway between 44th and 45th Streets). You may find that your hotel is quite close to one of these. Carey buses run every 30 mins from JFK, 6:00am-midnight. You needn't tip the bus driver.

Taxi: The cost of the trip to Manhattan is currently a flat fare of $30 excluding tolls ($3.50). One fare covers all passengers (maximum 4). It is customary to give the driver a 15% tip. You pay extra for large pieces of baggage.

LA GUARDIA

For domestic flights only. The airport is 8 miles outside Manhattan and driving time is about half an hour.

Bus: The **Carey Transport** bus drops passengers off near Grand Central Station and the Port Authority Bus Terminal (see Buses above) and costs $10.00. The bus serves the same four hotels mentioned above for an extra $1.50.

Taxi: Fares range between $20 and $30 (depending on how far into Manhattan you are going) plus $3.50 for tolls. Tipping (see above).

NEWARK

Newark is generally less crowded than JFK and everything moves much faster. Located 16 miles from Manhattan, it takes about 30-45 minutes to drive into the city.

Bus: Olympia Trails Airport Express. Service is between Newark airport and three locations in Manhattan: Penn Station (34th Street and Eighth Avenue), Grand Central (Park Avenue and 41st Street) and One World Trade Center (downtown). One-way fare is $7. You can also take **NJ Transit Number 300 Airport Express** to the Port Authority Bus Terminal (42nd Street and Eighth Avenue). Fare: one-way $7, round-trip $12.

Taxi: The average fare is about $35 plus $3.50 for tolls. (Includes a $10 surcharge over the metered fare.)

RAILROAD TERMINALS

All inter-city trains pass through **Pennsylvania (Penn) Station** (31st-33rd Streets at Seventh Avenue). Some commuter trains arrive at **Grand Central** (42nd Street and Park Avenue).

BUS TERMINALS

New York City's main bus terminal is the **Port Authority Bus Terminal** situated at 40th-42nd Streets on Eighth Avenue.

MANHATTAN STREET GEOGRAPHY

The island of Manhattan is bounded by the East River to the east and the Hudson to the west. It is separated from the Bronx at its northern end by the Harlem River.

Finding your way in Manhattan is really quite simple. Apart for the southern end of the island, the city's streets are laid out on a grid, which makes it virtually impossible to get lost.

- **Streets** run from east to west and are numbered on an ascending scale as you go north.
- **Avenues** run north to south and are mostly numbered from First to Twelfth, increasing in number from east to west.
- **Broadway** cuts across the grid moving westward as it snakes uptown.

Conventions to remember

- **Uptown** means north and **Downtown** means south
- **Crosstown** means east to west or vice versa;
- North of Washington Square, Fifth Avenue cuts the island into the **West Side** and the **East Side.**
- The area bounded by two streets or two avenues is called a **block**.

A few anomalies to note:

There are four extra avenues east of First Avenue below 14th Street named alphabetically from A to D, in a neighborhood commonly called Alphabet City.

There is no Fourth Avenue above 14th Street. Lexington, Park and Madison Avenues lie between Third and Fifth Avenues.

Avenue of the Americas, which is adorned with the coats-of-arms of North and South American countries, is the official name for Sixth Avenue. Still, most New Yorkers call it Sixth.

Above 59th Street, Eighth Avenue becomes Central Park

West, Ninth Avenue is called Columbus Avenue, 10th Avenue becomes Amsterdam Avenue and 11th Avenue is called West End Avenue. North of 110th Street, these avenues all have different names.

And then there is Broadway. Originally an old Native American trail, it's the oldest road across Manhattan. The triangular intersections of Broadway with other avenues are usually called squares.

The streets in areas such as the Financial District, Little Italy, Chinatown and the western part of Greenwich Village — the oldest part of Manhattan — have names instead of numbers, and do not follow a regular pattern.

GETTING AROUND

Always know the cross street or avenue of your destination. For example, the Empire State Building is on Fifth Avenue between 33rd and 34th streets.

Locating an Address

On the numbered streets, addresses increase consecutively from Fifth Avenue, to the east and to the west. Along the avenues, addresses increase consecutively going north.

To locate a street address the following table will help for the area between 14th and 59th Streets:

East Side

1-99	Fifth Avenue
100-199	Park Avenue
200-299	Third Avenue
300-399	Second Avenue
400-499	First Avenue
500-599	York Avenue

West Side

1-99	Fifth Avenue
100-199	Avenue of the Americas
200-299	Seventh Avenue
300-399	Eighth Avenue
400-499	Ninth Avenue
500-599	Tenth Avenue
600-699	Eleventh Avenue

How to find the approximate cross street of an avenue address:

Drop the last digit of the number, then divide the remaining number(s) by 2, then add or subtract the number shown on the chart below.

Avenues A-D	Add 3
1st Avenue	Add 3
2nd Avenue	Add 3
3rd Avenue	Add 10
4th Avenue	Add 8
Lexington Avenue	Add 22
Park Avenue	Add 34
Park Avenue South	Add 8
Madison Avenue	Add 26
5th Avenue up to 200	Add 13
up to 400	Add 16
up to 600	Add 18
up to 775	Add 20
775 to 1286	drop the last digit and subtract 18 (don't divide by two)
up to 1500	Add 45
above 2000	Add 24
Avenue of the Americas (6th)	Subtract 12
7th Avenue (below 110th St)	Add 12
7th Avenue (above 110th St)	Add 20
8th Avenue	Add 10
9th Avenue	Add 13
10th Avenue	Add 14
Amsterdam Avenue	Add 60
Broadway above 23rd St	Subtract 29
Central Park West	do not divide the number, add 60
Columbus Avenue	Add 60
Riverside Drive	do not divide the number, add 72
West End Avenue	Add 60

WALKING

New York is a pedestrian city and it's a folly to drive a car here. The best way to discover the city is on foot. At an average speed you can cover a short block in 1-2 mins. 20 short blocks make a mile. You will be amazed at how the city changes character from neighborhood to neighborhood, and sometimes even from block to block. And, walking is a good way to cruise men.

The city's two most prominent buildings — the Empire State and the twin towers of the World Trade Center (located on the southern tip of the island) are useful landmarks by which to orient yourself when exploring Manhattan by foot.

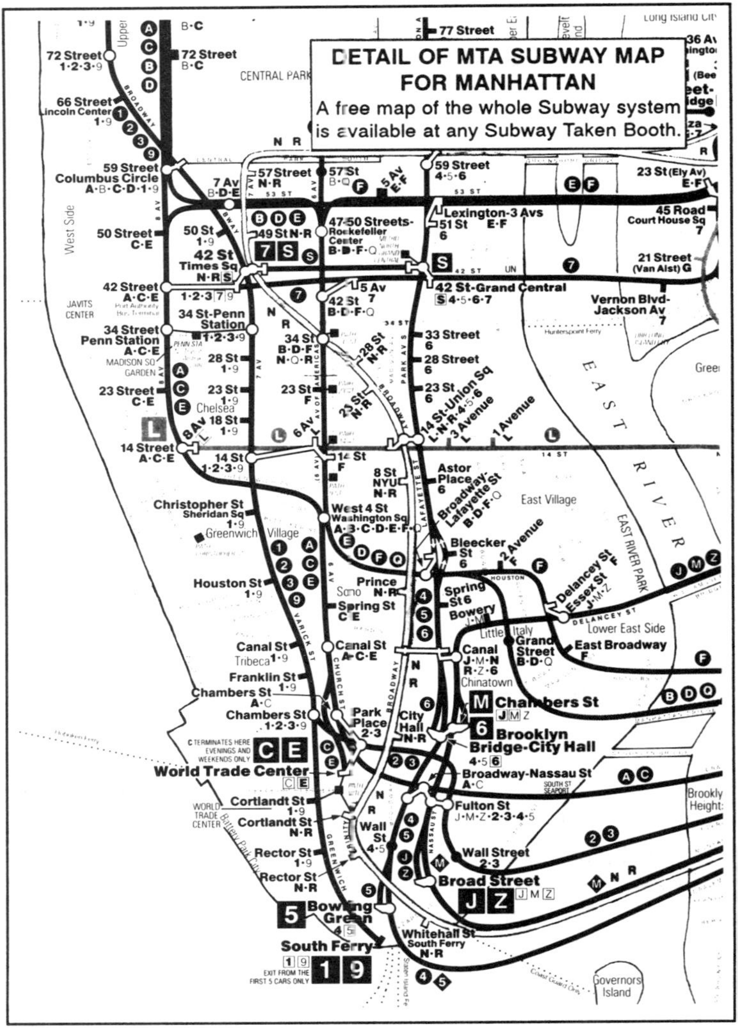

Map is current as of 1st June 1996. Copyright © New York Transit Authority. Used with the permition of MTA.

SUBWAY

There is much to complain about the subway system — it's often dirty and crowded — but it is without doubt the quickest way to get anywhere within Manhattan. It's a 24-hour, 7-day service that helps to make Manhattan an around-the-clock city. For a system that dates back to 1904, and one which copes with 3.5 million passengers every day, it is amazing the subway runs as well as it does. With 714 track miles and 469 stations in four boroughs, it's the world's largest urban railway. Don't be put off by the terrible reputation the subways seem to have outside New York. Much work is being done by the New York Transport Authority to keep the subways clean and safe. Many stations have been overhauled and trains are now graffiti-free.

A subway ride costs $1.50 for any distance. You need to buy tokens or the recently introduced MetroCards (magnetic fare cards) from the booths which are located in every station. Bills larger than $20 are not accepted and you are requested not to pay with pennies. If you buy tokens, it's advisable to buy more than one at a time, as this cuts down on your having to wait in long lines during rush hour.

It's best to refer to the trains by their letters or numerals. Don't be confused by the other names you may hear: the avenues the trains run under, and the initials IRT, IND and BMT, which date back to the days when independent companies operated separate train systems. And if you say blue line or green line people will know you're from out of town!

Subway maps are available free of charge at all token booths (see note under BUSES). The map will show you where to make free transfers between lines. Before you enter a turnstile make sure you are entering the platform for the direction you are going — uptown or downtown. It is only possible at few stations to cross over to the trains going in the opposite direction without having to pay another fare.

SUBWAY SAFETY

Enter the subway where you see a green light at the entrance. This indicates that the entrance is open and there is a 24-hour token sales clerk at that point. Red means closed or restricted entrance (no token booth). In the evenings, avoid entrances that are not properly lit — take the main, better-lit entrance around the block.

It's generally safe to travel by subway after dark, but wait for the train in the area close to the lighted booth where the token clerk sits. The booths are equipped with telephones for emergency situations. Most subways stations have an "After Hours Waiting Area" clearly marked with yellow signs. At night, when fewer passengers ride the trains, the safest car is the one near the center of the train with the conductor.

BUSES

Many New Yorkers prefer the buses to the subway, although buses generally take longer to get about in the city because of traffic jams and the occasional maddening waits caused by grid-lock. Still, if you have the time, it's a good way to see the city. In the evenings buses are often the quickest and safest means of transport. Bus routes go up and down the avenues and across town on the major two-way crosstown streets. Many routes are in operation 24 hours, though less frequently at night.

Bus fares are $1.50. You must have exact change in coins (no pennies accepted). You can also use a subway token or MetroCard. As you get in you can ask the driver for a transfer (valid for one hour), which will enable you to make one free ride on one of the intersecting routes designated on the transfer. You cannot use the transfers for the subway. Most of the buses are equipped for wheelchair access, and the driver can also make the bus "kneel" (lower the carriage closer to ground level) to help passengers who have difficulty mounting steps.

Free bus and subway maps are usually available at subway stations and also at tourist information centers (see below). Call New York City Travel Authority for travel information on buses and subways: ☎ (718) 330-1234 — 6:00am-9:00pm. (Non-English speaking customers: ☎ (718) 330-4847 — 7:00am-7:00pm). Long Island Railroad information: ☎ (718) 217-5477; Metro-North Railroad ☎ (1-800-638-7647) Merto-Info outside NYC and ☎ 532-4900 in NYC.

TAXIS

Cabs are the best way to get to places quickly, especially short distances at night (eg. bar hopping). Only use the licensed "medallion" taxis (yellow cabs) regulated by the New York City Taxi and Limousine Commission. You can hail these cabs on the streets or pick them up at taxi stands outside hotels and transportation terminals. Many taxi drivers are recent immigrants and their knowledge of English is often poor. Glance at a map and get an idea of where you have to go, because you may get a driver who is as new to the city as you are. On the other hand, you may get the old New York pro who will regale you with stories in non-stop Brooklynese. A light on the roof of the taxi indicates that it is available for hire. Off duty cabs have an "off duty" sign lit on their roof. There are almost 12,000 cabs in the city fleet but finding one on a rainy day is a fine art. This is when you find out just how aggressive and determined a New Yorker can be.

Taxi fares start at $2 and then jump 30¢ for each additional 1/5 mile (or 20¢ per minute stopped or in slow traffic). There is a surcharge of 50¢ between 8:00pm and 6:00am. Make sure the driver activates the meter the moment you get in. If you want a receipt, ask for it before the meter is shut off. One fare covers up to a maximum of four passengers. Most drivers will not take a fifth. You are not obliged to share cabs with strangers in this country. A tip of 10 to 15% (25¢ minimum) is customary but it's left to your discretion.

To report property lost in taxicabs ☎ (212) 840-4734, to make a complaint ☎ (212) 221-8294. Make sure you have the cab identification number which you will find on your receipt or listed next to the driver's identification plate on the right-hand side of the dashboard.

TELEPHONES

The area code for Manhattan is (212). Queens, Brooklyn, Staten Island and the Bronx are in the (718) area code. Calls within and between these two area codes are local calls. But if you are dialling from one region to the next you have to dial the area code prefixed by 1, just as you would for a long distance call.

Example, if you are in Manhattan and are calling someone in Brooklyn you have to dial 1-718 and the number.

A local call from a public pay phone costs 25 cents (one quarter) for the first three minutes. You must deposit more coins for each additional minute.

Calls to numbers with the area code (800) and (888) are toll-free (no charge).

The number for emergencies is 911 (no charge).

There is no shortage of public telephones in the city (at least a pair on every other block) although you'll find some of them broken. There are pay phones in many large building lobbies and in restaurants as well. With the exception of credit card phones, which you won't find on the street, all public pay phones are coin operated, so have plenty of change handy. You can now buy pre-paid phone cards at newspaper stands and corner stores. But although these cards offer very attractive rates per minute for overseas calls, be wary of a high surcharge per call.

Most public phones are operated by NYNEX (New York Telephone), the local phone company. From any of these phones you can receive directory information (including street addresses) free of charge by dialling 411. To speak to an operator dial 0. If you lose a quarter in the machine, you can ask the operator to refund the money to a phone number in the States. The other phone companies which operate public telephones on the streets of New York do not extend these courtesies and their phone service is often unreliable.

- Directory Inquiries — local: Dial 411; Outside New York: Dial the area code of the city and 555-1212.
- To find out the number of the phone you are using (especially at public phones where the number has been rubbed off): Dial 958.
- To find out the long distance carrier attached to the phone you are using: (700) 555-4141.

If no area code is given for the telephone numbers listed in this book, assume it is in the (212) area code and can be dialled direct within Manhattan.

CURRENCY

- 100 cents make a dollar.

Bills (notes): $1, $5, $10, $20, $50 and $100. All bills are the same color, green, and the same size.

Coins: 1¢ (penny), 5¢ (nickel) 10¢ (dime) 25¢ (quarter) and, occasionally, half-dollar. (Remember the dime is smaller than a nickel but worth more!)

BANKS are usually open from 9:00am to 3:00pm. Some may stay open later on one day of the week, and a few are open on Saturday mornings. Practically all the large banks are equipped with Automatic Teller Machines (ATMs) which are generally accessible 24 hours a day. You can use your American Express, Visa and Mastercard credit cards to get cash through many of these machines as well. You can also change your money and traveller's checks at most of the major banks.

EXCHANGE CENTERS (Business hours vary at each location; many are open on weekends)

American Express Travel Service: ☎ (800) 528-4800 for the location nearest to you. Branches include: World Trade Center (640-5130); New York Hilton (☎ 664-7798); Macy's Herald Square (☎ 695-8075); Bloomingdales (☎ 705-3171); JFK Airport (☎ 718/656-5673)

Chequepoint USA (☎ 980-6443)

Freeport Currencies (☎ 730-8339)

Harold Reuter and Co. Inc. (☎ 661-0826) or Toll Free within the US: ☎ (800) 258-0456; Grand Central Station (☎ 661-7600); Stern's Department Store (☎ 268-8517)

Thomas Cook Currency Service: Call the main office at Rockefeller Center (☎ 757-6915) for other locations.

POST OFFICES

Post offices are usually open from 9:00am to 5:30pm though a few may stay open later. Some are open on Saturdays from 9:00am to 1:00pm. The main post office is on Eighth Avenue between 31st and 33rd Streets and is open 24 hours, seven days a week.

PUBLIC TOILETS (RESTROOMS)

Do not expect to find toilets on the street. Once there were toilet facilities available at subway stations, but they have all been closed down. If you have a small bladder you must be creative and learn the locations of public restrooms in various hotels, department stores and gay bars. Toilets in restaurants are for customers only. A book titled *Where to Go: A Guide to Manhattan's Toilets*, is available in some bookstores if you are curious.

EMERGENCIES

- **Police, Fire and Ambulance: ☎ 911** (free call)

Deaf Emergency Teletypewriter for medical, fire and ambulance emergencies: ☎ (800) 342-4357.

All the major hospitals have 24-hour emergency rooms. The closest to the mid-town hotels is St. Luke's Roosevelt Hospital, 58th St./9th Avenue, ☎ 523-6800. St. Vincent's Hospital, 11th St./7th Avenue, ☎ 790-7997 serves Greenwich Village and Chelsea.

You can also try Manhattan Medical Care, 152 West 72nd St./ Columbus and Amsterdam Avenues, ☎ 496-9620, 8:00am-8:00pm (Mon-Fri), 10:00am to 6:00pm (Sat)

Emergency dentist (recorded listing of referrals): ☎ 679-3966

Victim Services Department (Travellers' Aid Society): ☎ 577-7777.

For US Residents only: The Travellers' Aid Service crisis intervention unit (☎ 944-0013) will help you get back in touch with your family or friends if you suddenly find yourself stranded in the city.

CRIME AND SAFETY

Stories about muggings and crime in New York get world-wide publicity, but you may be surprised to learn that this city ranks 13th in the U.S. in terms of per capita crime. And over the past two years there has been a dramatic decrease in violent crimes here. Of course, since New York is a street city, street crime is the most common and that makes everybody vulnerable. You cannot insure that you will never become a crime victim, so the best advice for someone who fears the worst is: **Don't be afraid, but always be careful.**

The safety tips below are based on advice from the New York Police Department Crime Prevention Department and the New York City Gay and Lesbian Anti-Violence Project (AVP). You may wonder how New Yorkers cope with life if they have to constantly look over their shoulders. But we call this developing street-smarts. In a very short time you'll be following these very practical, common-sense, precautions without any great effort, quite subconsciously

• Tourists are easy targets. Don't stand looking lost with an open map in hand and a camera dangling off your shoulder. Never flash about large wads of money. At banks, newspaper stands or shops, handle your cash and credit cards discreetly.

• When walking, stride purposefully, carrying yourself in a manner that indicates you are confident about where you are going, and that you are aware of others around you.

• Travel on well-lit streets Avoid short cuts through alleys. Walk against the traffic so a car cannot pull up unnoticed behind you. Do not approach a car to give directions. If you sense trouble, cross the street. Trust your instincts. It's better to be a little paranoid than to be naive.

• If you feel unsafe or threatened in any way remove yourself from the situation as quickly as possible. Run, make a noise, bang garbage cans, yell "FIRE!" You can carry a whistle to attract attention. Don't put up a fight if you are confronted with a weapon. New York City law prohibits the use of mace, tear-gas or such like self-defense weapons.

• Get to know where the nearest 24-hour establishments (grocery stores, newspaper stands) are located in the area in which you are staying.

• Never leave your valuables lying around unattended, ever. Avoid keeping your wallet in your rear trouser pocket.

• Stay clear of sidewalk card games. The most popular one is called Three-Card Monte. No matter how much you feel that Lady Luck is with you that day, you will never win!

• You may be accosted by panhandlers (beggars) on the streets of New York and less frequently on the subways. Separating the genuine cases from the con artists is never easy and you have to rely on your instincts and your generous inclinations. But don't be intimidated into giving anything if you don't want to. Politely and firmly say you are sorry and then adopt the classic New Yorker's way of looking into the middle distance — that seeing-without-seeing expression which prevents further bother.

• When riding the subway, if you have valuable packages avoid sitting in the seat next to the doors. In a crowded train, always be conscious of where your wallet is. If you feel somebody rubbing up against you, or a hand in your pocket (and I am not talking about a mutually pleasurable experience that two consenting strangers can enjoy in a crowded train), you might say loudly "Will the person who is doing that please stop!" By drawing attention without actual confrontation you may defuse a potentially dangerous situation.

• Before you board a bus always have your change or token ready. Be conscious of pickpockets who sometimes work in teams — one causes some distraction (like a staged argument) while the other snatches a bag or wallet. In another scam, someone will drop their change and you may kindly bend down to pick it up. Be nice, but watch your own bags.

To report a theft or a crime, locate the police precinct nearest you by calling ☎ 374-5000.

GAY-RELATED CRIME

As I have said before New York is a gay-friendly city and you will not be harassed by the police if you hold hands or kiss in public. But as we gain more visibility in the public eye, the backlash against gays and lesbians also increases, and anti-gay attacks occur. Be aware of the danger but don't let it get in the way of your enjoying your stay in New York.

• Try to leave bars, community centers and other gay/lesbian identified facilities with people who you know or trust. Assailants sometimes wait for potential victims outside of such places.

• Letting someone into your hotel room or apartment makes you vulnerable to robbery and assault. If you leave a bar with someone you've just met, introduce him to a friend or to the bartender. Let other people know you are leaving together. Let him think you have friends in the city, even if you don't. Many hotels ask for visitor's ID at the desk, which is a protection for you as well.

Don't be afraid to go to a police officer for help. For the most part the New York City police force, popularly known as "New

York's Finest," is sympathetic. They have come a long way since they raided gay bars twenty years ago and now undergo sensitivity training for handling gay issues. Openly gay officers have their own group called the Gay Officers Action League (G.O.A.L.). Discriminating against gays or lesbians in New York City is against the law. If you encounter harassment from a police officer, you can make note of the officer's name (worn under their badge) and report the incident.

The New York City Gay and Lesbian Anti-Violence Project provides advocacy, information and referrals for gay victims of crimes, whether they are gay-related or not.
24-hour hotline: ☎ 807-0187

TOURIST INFORMATION

THE NEW YORK CONVENTION & VISITORS BUREAU

2 Columbus Circle (Eighth Avenue and Broadway at 59th Street), New York, NY 10019
☎ 484-1200; Fax: 245-5943
24-hour hotline: ☎ (800) 692-8474
A multilingual staff provides free maps of the city, subway and bus maps and other useful literature. Open every day of the year, Mon-Fri, 9:00am-6:00pm; Weekends and holidays, 10:00am-3:00pm

I LOVE NEW YORK

New York State Department of Economic Development
51st Floor, 1515 Broadway
☎ 827-6250
Provides information on New York State as well as New York City.

NEWSPAPERS

There are three daily newspapers in New York. ***The New York Times***, referred to frequently as the "newspaper of record," is not only the city's premier publication, but the most influential paper in the country as well. For better or worse, many people regard *The Times* as the arbiter of cultural taste in the city, if not in the United States. By the way, folding *The Times* in four to read it while standing in the subway is an art which distinguishes the true New Yorker from the clumsy out-of-towner. Watch out though — the newsprint rubs off on your fingers!

The other two dailies, the ***New York Daily News*** and the ***New York Post*** are both tabloids and are everything that word implies: sensational headlines and racy news coverage with a conservative bent.

The *Wall Street Journal*, a national daily published in New York, is the bible of the business world. Two of the most popular alternative newspapers in New York are ***The Village Voice*** and ***New York Press*** which are both distributed free of charge. In the *Voice* look for Matt Groening's "Life in Hell" cartoons which depict the adventures of the nation's most famous same-sex cartoon couple, Jeff and Akbar. Reading the *Voice*'s Personals you'll also get an excellent cross-section view of New York's multisexual, multicultural singles world.

WEATHER

In this city of contrasts, the weather can blow hot and cold often in the space of the same week. January and February tend to be the coldest months. Snow falls from time to time and quickly turns into slush. July and August are the hottest and most unbearably humid months. New York is at its best September through December, with clear, crisp days, and in springtime (despite much rain) when the leaves bud. Summertime is, of course, the best time for boy-watching, and many New York boys dress quite shamelessly when the temperature rises!

Average Temperature in New York City, Fahrenheit (Celsius)

	Avg. Max	Avg. Min		Avg. Max	Avg. Min
January	38 (03)	26 (-03)	July	85 (29)	68 (20)
February	40 (04)	27 (-03)	August	84 (29)	67 (19)
March	49 (09)	34 (01)	September	77 (25)	60 (16)
April	61 (16)	44 (07)	October	66 (19)	50 (10)
May	72 (22)	53 (12)	November	54 (12)	41 (05)
June	80 (27)	63 (17)	December	42 (06)	31 (-01)

For up-to-date weather information ☎ 976-1212. It costs the same as a local call.

TIME

Local New York time (Eastern Standard Time) is five hours behind Greenwich Mean Time. On the first Sunday in April, the clocks are moved forward by an hour to observe Eastern Daylight Time (or Daylight Saving Time), which stays in effect through the last Sunday in October.

For the correct local time ☎ 976-1616, which costs the same as a local telephone call.

WHAT TO WEAR

New Yorkers dress very eclectically. Some dress up while others dress down. Apart from the expensive hotels, restaurants and exclusive clubs, you can wear pretty much what you want in any establishment. You won't go wrong with black for both evening and casual wear.

Always dress in layers. Many New York apartments are overheated, and it helps to shed a layer or two when you go indoors.

HOW TO UNDERSTAND THE NATIVES

Overseas visitors may encounter unfamiliar American words and phrases during their stay. New York-speak sometimes mystifies other Americans. Here is a glossary to make communication with the natives easy. You'll find more in other sections of the book as well.

African-American — Usually preferred over Black (do not say "Negro". Never say "Nigger," an unacceptable epithet — though some African-Americans use it within their own community.

Asian-American — preferred term over "oriental"

bangee boy — tough, "street-looking" African-American or Latino youth, often dressed in baggy jeans and wearing a baseball cap backwards

blast — a fabulous experience

bridge and tunnel crowd — a disparaging term for suburbanites, people who travel into Manhattan from the outer boroughs and New Jersey via the seven bridges and four tunnels into Manhattan

BYOB — Bring your own booze (or bottle)
dis (dissed) — to insult or show disrespect for (someone)
dive — a slightly seedy club
excuse me — this expression can be used very aggressively, often laden with heavy sarcasm, when trying to pick a quarrel with someone
fag hag — not very complimentary term for a straight woman who hangs out with gay men
femme — effeminate, opposite of butch
fierce — positive adjective indicating approval, eg. "that's real fierce drag!"; fabulous
friend of Dorothy — an old term meaning a fellow homosexual, refers to Dorothy in the Wizard of Oz
funky — adjective to indicate something or somebody with an edge, eg. funky clothes
hang, hang out — spend time idly at a certain place or with certain people
howyadoin'? - greeting, equivalent of Hi! doesn't require a literal response
in your face — not subtle, eg. the slogan "We're here! We're Queer! Get used to it!"
Latino and Latina — preferred by some over Hispanic
mary — campy term among queens, as in "Oh, Mary!"
maven — yiddish word for expert, used with an adjective, as in "theater maven"
Miss Thang! (Miss Thing!) — campy greeting, popular among drag queens
muscle queen — gay man who spends a lot of his time at the gym
Native American — preferred name for American Indians (never say "Red Indian")

oy vey!, oy gevalt!, oy! — Yiddishism indicating despair at something (literally meaning "Woe is me!"). Should be delivered with appropriate sigh and shake of head.
pissed (off) — angry
rip-off — to cheat
scam — a trick to cheat you
schlep — Yiddish meaning carry or drag (usually a heavy load)
schmuck — Yiddish for idiot
send up the river — to get into trouble, literally to send up the Hudson River to Sing-Sing prison in Ossining, New York.
sidewalk — pavement
sleaze bag — an untrustworthy, reprehensible character
stand on line — get in a queue (Note: New Yorkers never stand in line.)
subway — urban mass-transit rail system
Two Spirit — the Native American term for gays and lesbians
what'sup? — greeting, equivalent to Hi! Doesn't require a literal answer
yo! — greeting, equivalent to Hi! Can also be used aggressively to command attention
That and a dollar fifty will get you a ride on the subway! — a New Yorker's sarcastic response reminding you of the practicalities of a situation (the dollar amount changes according the current price of a subway token.)

Terms currently in vogue among homosexuals when referring to themselves: fag,homo, dyke (lesbians), 'mo;

The word "queer" covers gays and lesbians, bisexuals and transsexuals — but there is resistance to this word in some sections of the community.

New York City nicknames:

The Big Apple — used in the 1920s and 30s by people in the entertainment and sports worlds, particularly jazz musicians. Playing New York City meant making it Big Time: "There are many apples on the tree, but when you pick New York City you pick the Big Apple." The term was popularized in 1971 by a hugely successful tourist promotion campaign launched by the New York Convention and Visitors Bureau.

Gotham — made popular by the novelist Washington Irving and others in the early 19th century.

Knickerbocker — comes from the satire, *Knickerbocker's History of New York,* written by Washington Irving in 1809. The fictitious narrator of the book became so popular that his name became a term for New Yorkers of Dutch ancestry, and later for New Yorkers in general. It's the source for the name of the city's basketball team, The New York Knickerbockers ("The Knicks").

3: ACCOMMODATION

One of the costliest items of your stay in New York City will be accommodation. Be prepared to spend more than $100 per night at any decent hotel, even with special discount offers. And this excludes the hotel taxes which add up to a little over 13%. If you have set your sights on the glamorous hotels, think at least $250 per night. But since New York hotel rates are generally charged per room and not per person, it becomes more economical if you share.

You're in luck if you can stay with friends. But don't count on meeting the nice New Yorker who will invite you to share his apartment. Real estate is a high premium in this city, and many single people share tiny apartments, with one roommate sleeping on a sofa-bed in the living room. People here sometimes remain in domestic relationships merely to hold on to their apartment leases. If someone tells you "I can't ask you to my place because I am living with my ex-lover," he's probably telling you the truth.

Most of the guest houses listed below cater almost exclusively to the gay visitor and are slightly less expensive than the lower-range Manhattan hotels, but they do not always offer full services. The advantage is that you are in a gay environment and you will be able to get advice about New York gay life. And they'll take it for granted that you might bring a new friend to your place for the night.

CHELSEA INN

46 West 17th Street/ 5th & 6th Avenues, New York, NY 10011
☎ 645-8989; Fax: 645-1903
From $79 to $160
No breakfast, but most rooms have kitchenettes and refrigerators. Private baths in some rooms.
It isn't exclusively gay, but this European-style guesthouse (a renovated 19th century townhouse) is very gay friendly and is situated in the heart of gay Chelsea, right next door to the popular bar Splash.

CHELSEA MEWS GUEST HOUSE

344 West 15th Street/ 8th & 9th Avenues, New York, NY 10011
☎ 255-9174
From $65 to $150. No credit cards No breakfast. Most rooms without private bath. Limited services. Women not welcome.
A dark old 1840s town house; the rooms are furnished with the owner's antiques and objets d'art.

CHELSEA PINES INN

317 West 14th Street/ 8th Avenue New York, NY 10011
☎ 929-1023; Fax: 620-5456
From $59 to $89. All credit cards accepted. Continental Breakfast, color TV, air-conditioning/central heating, phone and refrigerator in room. Some rooms with private baths.
An 1850s brownstone which was "modernized" in the late 1930s and renovated in 1995. It is conveniently located on the border of Greenwich Village and Chelsea. Free coffee and cookies served all day.

COLONIAL HOUSE INN

318 West 22nd Street/ 8th Avenue, New York, NY 10011
☎ 243-9669; Fax: 633-1612
From $76 to $115 (Rates include taxes). No credit cards.
Continental Breakfast, color TV, air-conditioning, private phones, some rooms with fireplaces and refrigerators. Some rooms have private baths.
A renovated brownstone building situated in the historic district of Chelsea, close to the heart of the city. It is the only gay guest house with a 24-hour concierge.

INCENTRA VILLAGE HOUSE

32 Eighth Avenue/ West 12th Street, New York, NY 10014
☎ 206-0007
From $99 to $169. Most major credit cards accepted. No breakfast. Private baths and kitchenettes, private phones in all rooms. Limited services.
Elegantly furnished rooms situated in two red brick town houses. Twelve rooms, each named and decorated after different countries or states in which the owner has lived. Best for the visitor who is familiar with the city and likes a private home atmosphere.

THE NEW YORK BED AND BREAKFAST RESERVATION CENTER

☎ 977-3512

This service will place you in hosted (gay or gay-friendly) or unhosted apartments, studios and town-houses in Manhattan in the area of your choice. The rates are $60-90 per night, for a hosted apartment. An unhosted one-bedroom costs $100-150. If you are travelling with a companion you are better off selecting an unhosted venue.

• Among the non-gay, less-expensive (no frills) hotels you might consider the following:

BEACON HOTEL

2130 Broadway/ at 75th Street
New York, NY 10023
☎ 787-1100 or (800) 572-4969;
Fax: 724-0839
$115-$150

EDISON HOTEL

228 West 47th Street
New York, NY 10036
☎ 840-5000 or (800) 637-7070;
Fax: 719-9541
$95-$145

YMCA

• The YMCA provides cheap accommodation, and you can expect all the subversive thrills and all the discomforts the name implies. The great perk when staying at "The Y" is use of the gym and pool facilities. There are three YMCA branches in New York City. The most popular with gay men seems to be the West Side Y. But bear in mind, none of these establishments are exclusively gay:

YMCA, McBURNEY
206 West 24th Street
New York, NY 10011
☎ 741-9226; Fax: 741-0012
$32-$48

YMCA, VANDERBILT
224 East 47th Street
New York, NY 10017
☎ 756-9600; Fax: 752-0210
$49-$76

YMCA, WEST SIDE
5 West 63rd Street
New York, NY 10023
☎ 787-4400; Fax: 875-1334
$47-$57

• The NEW YORK CITY CONVENTION & VISITOR'S BUREAU will provide you with a free New York Hotel Guide upon request (see Chapter 2). The brochure lists over a hundred hotels with phone and fax numbers, and room rates.

4: CALENDAR

New York is never out of season. As actress Myrna Loy once said, "Something's always happening here. If you are bored in New York, it's your own fault."

For up to date information, refer to the events calendar published by the New York Convention and Visitors Bureau and weekly New York publications listed in Chapters 7 and 10. (All telephone numbers are in the (212) area code unless otherwise specified).

GAY EVENTS

(Refer also to the events highlighted in bold in the calendar listings below).

Gay Pride

The main gay event, of course, is the **Lesbian and Gay Pride March** which takes place during Gay Pride Weekend, the last weekend in June. It commemorates the Stonewall uprising, the symbolic beginning of the gay rights movement. Hundreds of thousands of gay men, lesbians and well-wishers march down Fifth Avenue, the City's premier parade route, which is painted with a lavender stripe for the occasion. The March ends on Christopher Street. A day-long street fair, **Pride Fest**, is held along the waterfront at the foot of Christopher St. In the evening the **Annual Pride Dance** is held on a bulkhead built alongside the Hudson River. The Dance (one of several Gay Pride parties in the city) commences and concludes with spectacular firework displays.

photo copyright © Tina Paul **GAY PRIDE PARADE**

Circuit Parties

Visitors from all over the world come to New York for the four **Saint-at-Large** parties, which carry on the bacchanalian traditions of the Saint, a legendary New York disco which closed in 1988. The most popular is the notoriously raunchy **Black Party,** which is held in the last weekend in March. Veteran party queens take a "disco nap" in the evening and arrive at the Black Party dressed in their scanty best only after 1am. (The party usually continues well into the next day.) Also keep in mind *The Morning Party* hosted by the Gay Men's Health Crisis in August on Fire Island.

Wigstock

You ain't seen hairpieces until you've been to this outdoor drag festival hosted by The "Lady" Bunny. It all started with a handful of inebriated drag queens singing and carrying-on in a derelict East Village park in 1984. Now Wigstock is one of New York's major queer events. It's been celebrated on film (*Wigstock: The Movie*) and has spawned a clone in San Francisco. Don't be shy about dressing up for the occasion; the wigs in the audience are often more outrageous than those on stage. Performances by New York's drag superstars Lypsinka and RuPaul and the high camp rock band Dee Lite are among the crowd pleasers every year. Having outgrown the small park in Tompkins Square where it began, the ever-popular drag extravaganza is now held on the Hudson River waterfront near Christopher Street.

WIGSTOCK photo copyright © Tina Paul

JANUARY

Ice Capades, Madison Square Garden, ☎ 465-6000

The Winter Antiques Show, Seventh Regiment Armory, Park Avenue at 67th Street, ☎ 439-0300

FEBRUARY

The White Party (The Saint-at-large), President's Day weekend, ☎ 674-8541

Chinese New Year, Fireworks in Chinatown

Black History Month, ☎ 722-9534

The Art Show, New York Armory

Westminster Kennel Club Dog Show, Madison Square Garden, ☎ 465-6000

MARCH

New York Flower Show, Pier 92

The International Cat Show, Madison Square Garden, ☎ 465-6000

New York City Gay Men's Chorus, Pops Concert, ☎ 924-7770

St. Patrick's Day Parade (Note: for past several years the organizers have been distinctly gay unfriendly causing much controversy in the city)

Ringling Brothers, Barnum and Bailey Circus, Madison Square Garden, (March-May), ☎ 861-2100

Night of 1,000 Gowns, ☎ 475-0838. Annual drag ball organized by the Imperial Court of New York (see Chapter 7)

The Black Party (The Saint-at-large) last weekend in March, ☎ 674-8541

APRIL

Easter Parade, 5th Avenue, Easter sunday

Easter Show, Radio City Music Hall, ☎ 247-4777

Easter Bonnet Competition (Broadway Cares/Equity Fights AIDS fundraiser), ☎ 840-0770

Macy's Spring Flower Show, ☎ 560-4060

New York Leather Weekend and Mr. Leather Contest, ☎ 228-2706

Spring Flower Show, New York Botanical Garden, Bronx, ☎ (718) 220-8700

Sakura Matsuri (Cherry Blossom Festival), Brooklyn Botanical Garden, ☎ (718) 622-4433

MAY

AIDS Walkathon, Gay Men's Health Crisis, ☎ 337-1913

Fleet Week — when sailor boys roam the city. Call Intrepid Museum ☎ 245-2533 for various naval events

Ninth Avenue International Food Festival, ☎ 581-7217

Washington Square Park Outdoor Art Show, Memorial Day weekend (also Labor Day weekend)

American Arts and Crafts Festival, Lincoln Center

Ukrainian Festival, 7th street, between 2nd and 3rd Avenues

JUNE

The New York Lesbian and Gay Film Festival, ☎ 254-7228

Gay Pride Weekend, Pride Rally, Pride Fest, Annual Pride Dance, ☎ 807-7433, last weekend in June

AIDS Candlelight March, ☎ (718) 565-6789 Held on the Friday of Gay Pride Weekend. The silent march starts at Sheridan Square and proceeds to St. Veronica's Church for an Interfaith Celebration of Remembrance. After the Service the march proceeds down Christopher Street to the Hudson River for a "burial at sea" of flowers and candles.

New York City Gay Men's Chorus, Gay Pride Concert, ☎ 924-7770

Metropolitan Opera free performances in the city parks (June-July), ☎ 362-6000

New York Philharmonic free concerts in the city parks (June-July), ☎ 875-5656

Puerto Rican Day Parade

JVC Jazz Festival, Carnegie Hall and other venues, ☎ 787-2020

Mermaid Parade, Coney Island, Brooklyn, ☎ (718) 373-5159

JULY

Macy's Fireworks Celebrations (Independence Day), ☎ 560-4400

Free theater in Central Park New York Shakespeare Festival (July-Aug) , ☎ 598-7100

Bastille Day Celebrations, Florent Restaurant, ☎ 989-5779. Good food and queer performances to celebrate the French National Day on the Sunday following July 14.

AUGUST

GMHC's The Morning Party, The Pines, Fire Island, ☎ 337-1913. Held on the third Sunday in August.

Lincoln Center Out of Doors, performing arts festival

Harlem Week, street fairs, gospel festivals and cultural events, ☎ 427-7200

Greenwich Village Jazz (Aug-Sept)

US Open Tennis Championships, National Tennis Center, Flushing Meadows, Queens, ☎ (718) 271-5100

SEPTEMBER

Feast of San Gennaro Street Festival, Mulberry St., Little Italy, ☎ 226-9546

Wigstock, Labor Day

New York Film Festival, Lincoln Center, ☎ 875-5050

New York is Book Country bookfair, 5th Avenue, ☎ 522-3074

The Broadway Flea Market (Broadway Cares/Equity Fights AIDS fundraiser), ☎ 840-0770

New York Lesbian and Gay Experimental Film/Video Festival, ☎ 925-5883.

West Indian American Day Carnival, Crown Heights, Brooklyn, ☎ (718) 774-8807

OCTOBER

National Coming Out Day (October 11), ☎ (800) 445-6263

Columbus Day Parade, Fifth Avenue, ☎ 249-9923

Feast of St. Francis, Blessing of the animals, Cathedral of St. John the Divine

International Antiques Show, Seventh Regiment Armory, Park Avenue, ☎ 439-0300

Halloween Parade in Greenwich Village (once the most outrageous gay parade, but now very mixed)

The Saint-at-Large Halloween Party, ☎ 674-8541

NOVEMBER

New York Marathon (through all five boroughs of New York), ☎ 860-4455

GMHC Danceathon, Gay Men's Health Crisis, Jacob Javits Center, ☎ 337-1913

The Fall Flower Show, New York Botanical Garden, Bronx, ☎ (718) 220-8700

Gypsy of the Year Competition (Broadway Cares/Equity Fights AIDS), ☎ 840-0770

Macy's Thanksgiving Day Parade, ☎ 290-5432

DECEMBER

Day without Art and **Night Without Light**, December 1, World AIDS Day, ☎ 206-6758

Holiday store window displays: Lord & Taylor, Saks, Barney's Department Store, Nov-Jan

Holiday Spectacular, Radio City Music Hall, Nov-Jan

Lighting of Giant Christmas Tree, Rockefeller Center, ☎ 698-8676

New York City Gay Men's Chorus, Holiday Concert, ☎ 924-7770

The Nutcracker by the New York City Ballet, Lincoln Center, ☎ 870-5570

NEW YEAR'S EVE

Runner's World Midnight Run in Central Park, ☎ 860-4455

Fireworks over East River, South Street Seaport, Piers 16 & 17, ☎ 669-9400; Fireworks at Prospect Park, Brooklyn

New Year's Eve at Times Square

Saint-at-Large New Year's Eve Party, ☎ 674-8541

IMPORTANT NEW YORK SEASONS

American Ballet Theater (April-June), Lincoln Center, ☎ 362-6000

New York City Ballet (Nov-Feb), Lincoln Center, ☎ 870-5570

New York City Opera (July-Oct), ☎ 870-5570

Metropolitan Opera (Sept-April), Lincoln Center, ☎ 362-6000

New York Philharmonic (Sept-June) Avery Fisher Hall, Lincoln Center, ☎ 875-5030

Carnegie Hall (Sept-June)

New York Mets baseball (April-Oct), Shea Stadium, Queens, ☎ (718) 507-6387

New York Yankees baseball (April-Sept), Yankee Stadium, Bronx, ☎ (718) 293-4300

New York Knicks basketball (Nov-April) Madison Square Garden, ☎ 861-2100

PUBLIC HOLIDAYS

New Year's Day; Martin Luther King Day (Monday following Jan 15); President's Day (3rd Monday in February); Easter; Memorial Day (last Monday in May); Independence Day (July 4); Labor Day (first Monday in September); Columbus Day (2nd Monday in October); Veteran's Day (November 11); Thanksgiving (4th Thursday in November); Christmas Day

5: MANHATTAN HISTORY & SIGHTS

It's only 14 miles long, but it will take more than a single visit to get fully acquainted with Manhattan. In fact, it will take more than this single chapter to do the island justice. One way to learn the geography of Manhattan is to take the Circle Line cruise which circumnavigates the island in three hours (details at the end of this chapter). For the best New York experience explore Manhattan's neighborhoods on foot as much as you can. Remember, try not to do too much in a single day!

In this chapter I'll point out Manhattan's best-known landmarks and neighborhoods, travelling from south to north, in the direction in which the city expanded historically. We'll also be moving back and forth from east to west as we proceed uptown. Phone numbers appear in parenthesis, and unless otherwise indicated, are in the 212 area code.

COLONIAL NEW YORK

European knowledge of the North American coastline began with the voyages of Giovanni da Verrazano, an Italian explorer working for Francis I of France in 1524; Esteban Gómez who explored in the name of King Charles V of Spain in 1525; and, most notably, the Englishman Henry Hudson, sailing for the Dutch East India Company in 1609. Hudson was seeking a water route to China when he sailed up the river that now bears his name.

In the sixteen years after Hudson's trip, the Dutch West India Company made various settlements along the coast. In 1625 they established New Amsterdam on the southern tip of the island which the local Algonquin tribes called *Man-a-hat-a.* The following year, according to legend, Peter Minuit, the first Governor General of New Amsterdam, clinched the first of this city's lucrative real-estate deals by purchasing the entire 14-mile island for goods valued at 60 guilders (calculated by 19th century historians as $24).

Early New Amsterdam was a fur trading post which thrived despite its notoriously unruly bunch of colonists and conflicts with various local Native American tribes. Governor Peter Stuyvesant, who took office in 1647, finally established order, albeit ruthlessly, in the fledgling city. In 1653 he built a fortified wooden wall from river to river along the path of what is now Wall Street. According to some historians the wall was built to keep hostile Indian tribes out of the city, but others believe it was protection against attacks by the British, who were the trading rivals of the Dutch.

Nonetheless, in 1664 the British captured New Amsterdam and renamed it for the Duke of York, brother to King Charles II. The Dutch briefly recaptured New York in 1673 and rechristened it New Orange. In 1674, the name reverted to New York after the settlement became British again under the Treaty of Westminster. Although the thirteen American colonies declared their independence from Britain in 1776, British forces occupied all of present-day New York for the entire duration of the seven-year Revolutionary War. In 1784 New York became the first capital of the new nation, and in 1789, George Washington took his oath as the first President of the United States in Federal Hall on Wall Street. New York remained the nation's capital until the seat of government was moved to Philadelphia in 1790.

DOWNTOWN
(Below 14th Street)

The Statue of Liberty, which stands on Liberty Island in New York Harbor, is perhaps the most famous landmark of the entire United States. Dedicated in 1886, it is internationally recognized as a symbol of democratic freedom. The 151 foot statue, designed by Frederic Auguste Bartholdi, was a gift from the people of France. Liberty's friendly beacon was the first sight that greeted the waves of immigrants that flowed through New York harbor during the first half of this century, making New York the richly diverse city it is today. In her famous poem, Emma Lazarus captures the spirit of the Statue with the following verse:

> Give me your tired, your poor,
> Your huddled masses yearning to breathe free,
> The wretched refuse of your teeming shore.
> Send these, the homeless, tempest-tost to me,
> I will lift my lamp beside the golden door!

To get to the Statue you take a ferry from Battery Park, next door to the Staten Island Ferry Terminal (☎ 269-5755). The boat also takes you to the **Ellis Island National Monument** (through which nearly 16 million immigrants passed between 1892-1924) and the **Ellis Island Museum of Immigration** (☎ 363-3200) which houses exhibits tracing the migration to America of more than 100 ethnic groups. For Statue of Liberty and Ellis Island visiting hours ☎ 363-3200. You can climb to the top of the Statue (lines are long, especially in the summer), or you can cruise past it on the Staten Island Ferry (see Chapter 14).

Lower Manhattan

The narrow streets and alleyways in this, the oldest, section of Manhattan are reminders of the size and scale of colonial New York, although the **Financial District** is now squished into this small area. Over the years the shoreline of Manhattan was extended with landfills. Pearl Street, for example, was so named because it runs along what was once an East River shore covered with pearly shells. Lower Manhattan is busy during the day but empties out by evening. Tourists have the place to themselves on weekends.

Battery Park is named after the row of cannon that once defended the old New York shoreline (now State Street). You get excellent views of New York Harbor and the Statue of Liberty from here. The fortress in the park is the **Castle Clinton National Monument** (☎ 344-7220 for visitor information) which dates to 1811. Originally called the West Battery, it was renamed after De Witt Clinton, a famous mayor of the city as well as governor of the state. Castle Clinton was later converted into a theater, where in 1850, the great showman P.T. Barnum staged the American debut of Jenny Lind, the "Swedish Nightingale".

At the intersection of Battery Place and State Street stands the former U.S. Customs House, a Beaux Arts masterpiece completed in 1907, and now the home of the **National Museum of the American Indian**. To its north is Bowling Green, said to be the site of Peter Minuit's famous transaction, then a Dutch cattle market and eventually the city's first park.

Fraunces Tavern (☎ 425-1778), a 20th century reconstruction of an 18th century brick building where George Washington bade farewell to his troops in 1783, stands at the intersection of Broad and Pearl Streets. Walking east to the river you'll find the **Vietnam Veterans Plaza**, which houses a glass memorial wall dedicated to the soldiers who died in that war.

It is hard to believe that **Wall Street**, the hub of the world famous financial center, was once the northern limit of New Amsterdam. This is the site of Governor Stuyvesant's wood fortification, which was torn down in 1699. The **New York Stock Exchange** was formed here in 1792. For free tickets to watch trading from the 3rd floor gallery of the current Stock Exchange (visitor's entrance at 20 Broad Street) ☎ 656- 5167. Several major banks and financial institutions are headquartered cheek by jowl in the Wall Street area. The **Federal Reserve Bank**, located at 33 Liberty Street, is a Renaissance-style edifice modelled on the Strozzi Palace in Florence. You can tour the underground vaults in which many nations store gold. Admission is free but reservations must be made a week in advance ☎ 720-6130.

The nerve center of international trade and commerce in New York is, of course, the **World Trade Center**. Dominating the New York skyline, the 1,350 foot tall, twin towers are the tallest buildings in the city. From the observation deck on the 107th floor of the southern tower (Two World Trade Center), which is open till 11:30 pm, you get breath-taking views of New York Harbor, New Jersey and Long Island (☎ 435-7397).

In a remarkable recycling enterprise, the soil and rock excavated to dig the foundation of the World Trade Center was used to create one of the most impressive pieces of recent urban development. **Battery Park City**, built on 92 acres of landfill in the Hudson River, is Manhattan's newest neighborhood. It houses the **World Financial Center,** several office and apartment complexes, and also provides the best public space in Lower Manhattan, bordered by a pleasant (and often cruisy) esplanade along the Hudson.

The **South Street Seaport Museum** (☎ 669-9424) is a popular, crowded tourist attraction. A collection of historic buildings, restored ships, museums and shopping malls, it celebrates the 19th century maritime history of New York, when South Street was known as the "Street of Ships". You also get a fantastic view of the Brooklyn Bridge from here. Nearby is the **Fulton Fish Market**, established in 1821 and still active from midnight to dawn. ☎ 669-9416 if you are interested in taking the guided bi-weekly tours at 6.00 in the morning.

There are several other noteworthy sights in Lower Manhattan. The **Federal Hall National Memorial** (☎ 264-8711), located at 26 Wall Street, which was built in 1842, marks the site where George Washington took his oath as President in 1789. The **Woolworth Building** (233 Broadway near Park Place) was erected in 1913 and was, for a brief time, the tallest building in the world. The magnificent gothic skyscraper was nicknamed the "Cathedral of Commerce" and served as the headquarters for Frank Woolworth's famous chain of stores. Check out its gloriously ornate and picturesque lobby. The seat of New York City government is the elegant Federal-style **City Hall** which was built in 1802-11. The historic **Trinity Church** and **St. Paul's Chapel** (in continuous use since 1776) are nearby. Finally, when you are in Lower Manhattan don't forget to walk across the spectacular **Brooklyn Bridge**.

Chinatown and Little Italy

Most visitors come to **Chinatown** for the food, and indeed there is no better place in New York for authentic Chinese cuisine. This bustling community was established by Chinese immigrants in the 1870s. Start at Chatham Square and explore Mott, Bayard and Pell Streets. The telephone booths are shaped like little pagodas and the sounds of Cantonese and other dialects fill the air. Sundays are the busiest. For the Chinese New Year, which falls on the first full moon after January 19, the entire neighborhood is thronged with crowds celebrating with firecrackers.

Traditionally, Canal Street formed the northern border of Chinatown. Now, however, you'll see many Chinese owned establishments north of Canal, in the neighborhood known as **Little Italy**. Mulberry Street is Little Italy's main drag. Immigrants, primarily from Southern Italy, moved in here between 1880 and 1924. Today, though the Italian population of this district is no longer the majority, the local restaurants and cafes may remind you of *The Godfather* movies or a film by Martin Scorsese. The area comes vividly to life for the festivals of San Gennaro (on Mulberry Street in late September) and St. Anthony (on Sullivan Street in mid June).

The Lower East Side

The area north of Chinatown and extending to East River is inextricably tied with the histories of the immigrant populations of New York. At one time the Lower East Side provided refuge to a large number of Irish people who fled the potato famines of 1846-1860, and contained Kleindeutschland (Little Germany) as well. But it is primarily associated with Eastern European Jews who arrived in their greatest numbers between 1881 and 1914. The **Lower East Side Tenement Museum** (☎ 431-0233), at Orchard and Broome Streets, is located in a restored 1863 tenement which at times housed immigrants from over twenty-five different countries. Also visit the nearby **Eldridge Street Synagogue** built by Polish Jews in 1886. **Orchard Street** is a bargain hunter's paradise (now particularly for leather goods), although pushcart vendors no longer crowd this street as they did in the old days.

The Bowery, an old Indian trail, was once part of Peter Stuyvesant's *bouwerie*, the Dutch word for farm. In the mid 19th century New York's glittering theater district was located on this wide avenue. After its heyday, the Bowery became a skid row with cheap lodgings and cheap liquor, and for a long time the name was synonymous with the poor and the forsaken. At the corner of the Bowery and Grand Street stands the **Bowery Bank** (now **GreenPoint Bank**), a superb piece of 1894 architecture by the renowned New York firm of McKim, Mead and White.

SoHo

The name stands for *So*uth of *Ho*uston Street. Although fashionable in the 1840s, this area degenerated into what was considered a commercial slum and was targeted for demolition in the early 1960s. Instead SoHo was rejuvenated by artists who were attracted by the cheap rents and huge loft spaces. These buildings, most of which date from 1860 to 1890, are the best examples of cast-iron architecture in the United States. In 1973 the creation of the **SoHo Historic District** ensured the protection of a 26-block tract between West Broadway, Houston (which New Yorkers pronounce "house-ton"), Canal and Crosby Streets. SoHo now houses many trendy art galleries, boutiques and restaurants which have priced out many of the very artists who rejuvenated the area. Among the finest SoHo edifices are the **Puck Building** (Lafayette and E. Houston Streets) dating from 1885, and the **Haughwout Building** (490 Broadway at Broome Street), an impressive palazzo built in 1857, sometimes called "The Parthenon of Cast-Iron Architecture".

TriBeCa

The acronym stands for *Tri*angle *Be*low *Ca*nal Street. Once a warehouse district, this is another downtown area that has been transformed by the influx of artists, fashionable restaurants and galleries. Actor Robert De Niro recently set up the **TriBeCa Film**

Center at 375 Greenwich Street and the **TriBeCa Grill**, of which he is part owner, is one of the trendiest restaurants in the city.

Greenwich Village

The population of Greenwich Village exploded in the 1790s when large numbers of New Yorkers fled to what was then open pasture in the wake of a series of yellow-fever outbreaks. There aren't many skyscrapers or high-rises in the Village because the island's volcanic bedrock lies deeper below the surface here than in most other places. The geography of Greenwich Village is a tangle of streets following the routes of old cattle paths and river trails that remained intact when Manhattan's grid system was laid out in 1811. Wander around (with a map) and you will come across quaint townhouses along the

SUBWAY SCENE photo copyright © Stephen DiMenna

tree-lined side streets, a refreshing break from the skyscrapers of mid and lower Manhattan.

Greenwich Village was the bohemian center of New York earlier in this century. Now quite popular with tourists (and straight suburban teenagers) the Village is nonetheless the traditional center of gay New York, and still houses most of the city's gay bars and institutions. These days, however, you may find as many gay men and gay venues in neighboring Chelsea.

The gayest section of Greenwich Village is the **West Village**. Every gay visitor must visit **Christopher Street**, the birthplace of the modern gay and lesbian rights movement. The city has renamed the section of Christopher Street between 6th and 7th Avenues **Stonewall Place** in commemoration of the riots which took place here at a bar called Stonewall Inn in 1969. Nearby **Gay Street**, with its well preserved set of Greek revival and Federal-style houses, was not named for the gay community; the name most probably comes from an 18th century family which lived there. Walk west to the foot of Christopher Street at the Hudson River and check out the piers, which were once the prime playground for the community. Gay men still flock to these now rotting wooden structures for sunbathing and cruising.

Other points of interest in the West Village include the **Gansevoort Market** in the city's meat-packing district (bound by Gansevoort and 14th Streets, Ninth Avenue and the Hudson River). In the mid-19th century this was the location of the Gansevoort Docks, where Herman Melville, author of *Billy Budd* and *Moby Dick*, spent 19 years as a customs inspector. After dark, the meat-market area attracts both the city's trendy set and its demi-monde. Don't wander about alone late at night.

STONEWALL

"Remember Stonewall!" is the rallying call for gay liberation around the world. It commemorates *the* symbolic event of the modern gay and lesbian movement: three days of street protests that erupted in response to a police raid on a Greenwich Village gay bar in 1969. The actual sequence of events during the early hours of June 28, at the Stonewall Inn on Christopher Street, may never be fully unravelled. The riots began when eight officers entered the bar on a routine raid expecting to harass the patrons and make a few arrests. Instead they found themselves besieged by a crowd of over 300 people taunting them and attacking them with beer cans, bottles and showers of coins. Black and Hispanic drag queens at the forefront bore the brunt of police brutality and homophobia. Was the riot ignited by a cross-dressed lesbian, who fought back as she was hauled away by the police? Did Judy Garland's funeral the previous afternoon fuel the angry mood of the crowd? Some credit a full moon for that night's disturbances. What matters is that the cops were confronted with unprecedented defiance from gay people.

The Stonewall rebellion was certainly not the first protest against the laws that made gay people social outcasts and criminals. The incipient gay liberation movement gathered momentum during the Civil Rights battles of the 1960 s. But Stonewall was a dramatic and violent confrontation in the struggle for homosexual rights, and is a historical marker for that moment which galvanized gay people throughout the country. New York celebrates Stonewall every year with Gay and Lesbian Pride Weekend festivities and the Lesbian and Gay Pride March along Fifth Avenue.

For more on Stonewall and its legacy, see gay historian Martin Duberman's book *Stonewall*, which contains a comprehensive account of the riots and their aftermath.

'GAY LIBERATION' at Christopher Park, photo copyright © Stephen DiMenna

The heart of Greenwich Village is **Washington Square Park**. Originally an Indian hunting ground traversed by a stream called Minetta Brook, it was a potter's field and later a public execution ground until it became a park in 1827. On the north side of the park is the **Washington Arch**. Initially a wooden structure erected to commemorate the centennial of George Washington's inauguration as President, it was rebuilt in marble in 1895. The Federal style row houses across the street from the arch are reminders of the area's 19th century elegance, the world of Henry James' novel *Washington Square*. The buildings of the **New York University** campus surround the park, and the famous Provincetown Playhouse, where Eugene O'Neill first produced his work in New York, is located on nearby MacDougal Street.

Greenwich Village, which has been home to many famous people, contains far too many sites of historic interest to cover in this brief account. If you are interested in a detailed history of the Village and its residents see *The Greenwich Village Guide* by Fred W. McDarrah and Patrick J. McDarrah.

The East Village

The ambience of the East Village is very different from that of the West Village. It's home to an eclectic mix of Ukrainian, Polish and Russian immigrants, a large Latino population, young gay activists, artists, bohemians, anarchists and even a few left-over hippies. Certain areas of the East Village have lately undergone gentrification, while other areas have retained their seedy character. In the 60s, the East Village was the epicenter of the counter-culture movement, and in the 70s, the emerging punk movement.

Touristy **St. Mark's Place** is the historical center of the East Village. In the 1950s Jack Kerouac, William Burroughs, Allen Ginsberg and Norman Mailer, members of the famous "Beat Generation" lived here. The building at No 6, now a popular video store, was the home of James Fenimore Cooper, author of *The Last of the Mohicans*, in 1834. Gay men will remember the Cooper house as the site of the St. Mark's Baths, which, until it was shut down in the early 80s, was one of the most popular gay bathhouses in the city.

10th and 11th Streets between Second and Third Avenues comprise the **St. Mark's Historic District**, where **St. Mark's-in-the-Bowery**, the second oldest church in the city, is located. It was built in 1799 on the probable site of Governor Peter Stuyvesant's chapel. In the churchyard you'll find a memorial plaque for gay English poet W. H. Auden, who lived in this neighborhood.

In the mid-19th century, wealthy New York families such as the Astors, Vanderbilts and Delanos lived in houses near Lafayette Street, Great Jones Street and Astor Place. The **Old**

Merchant's House, an 1830s brick townhouse that belonged to a wealthy merchant, stands at 29 East 4th Street, between Lafayette Street and Bowery (☎ 777-1089). The interiors and furnishings are preserved just as they were when its owner lived there.

At East 7th Street (near 3rd Avenue) stands **Cooper Union**, an Italianate style edifice built by multi-millionaire Peter Cooper in 1859 to house the country's first co-educational college open to all races and creeds. Cooper Union's Great Hall has hosted many debates on the critical issues of the day. In 1860, Abraham Lincoln gave a famous speech that guaranteed him the Presidential nomination that year. Organizations such as the American Red Cross and the NAACP, the Black civil rights organization, were started here. In more recent times, ACT-UP, the AIDS activist direct-action group, held its highly provocative weekly meetings at this venue.

The **Joseph Papp Public Theater**, near Cooper Union on Lafayette Street, is the home of the New York Shakespeare Festival. It was built between 1849 and 1881 for the Astor Library, whose collection of books formed the nucleus of the New York Public Library System in 1912.

From the turn of the century up until about 1930, Second Avenue from Houston to 14th Streets was the home of the Yiddish theater. Today nothing remains of the *Jewish Rialto*, as it was then called, expect for a few dairy restaurants and kosher delicatessens in the area, the Orpheum Theater (1908), currently a popular off-Broadway theater, and the East Village Cinema complex, a converted Yiddish playhouse that retains some of its original decor.

On Second Avenue near 12th Street you'll find the **Ukrainian Museum** (☎ 288-0110). Various Polish and Ukrainian restaurants and institutions are located nearby. The **Tenth Street Baths** (☎ 473-8806) on 268 East 10th Street, which dates back from the late 19th century, is the only traditional Russian-Turkish bathhouse in the city. It's well worth a visit just to experience a traditional Russian platza rub (oak branches), but remember this is not a gay establishment!

More than a dozen Indian restaurants are concentrated on the block of East 6th Street between First and Second Avenues. **Little India**, or Curry Row, as it is more colloquially called, is your best bet for authentic and inexpensive Indian cuisine in Manhattan.

Alphabet City is named for the four avenues, A to D, located between First Avenue and the East River from 14th to Houston Streets. Its Spanish-speaking residents call it *Loisaida*. Until recently the neighborhood was heavily drug infested and unsafe. It is now going through a gentrification process and is home to many young gay New Yorkers who live alongside the several older immigrant communities. A trendy young crowd hangs out on Avenue A between 4th and 14th Streets where some of the city's better and quite inexpensive restaurants and coffee houses are located. You'd be well advised, however, not to wander east of Avenue B after dark. The centerpiece of Alphabet City is the 16-acre **Tompkins Square Park**, which has undergone an extensive facelift. Wigstock, the queer community's drag festival, originated here, but now the popular annual event is held on the piers of the West Village.

MID-MANHATTAN
(14th to 59th Streets)

Many people contend that **Chelsea** is more gay than the adjoining West Village. The area between 14th and 23rd Streets on 7th, 8th and 9th Avenues is home to trendy young gay men and several popular restaurants and gay establishments. Take a stroll on 8th Avenue and you may make new friends.

The **Hotel Chelsea** (☎ 243-3700) on West 23rd Street, between 7th and 8th Avenues, is a neighborhood landmark. Not a luxury hotel by any standard, this charming but ramshackle 1883 apartment building is steeped in literary history. Dylan Thomas, Arthur Miller, Quentin Crisp, Thomas Wolf, Mary McCarthy, Virgil Thompson, and Vladimir Nabokov, to name only a few, all lived here; in these rooms William Burroughs wrote *The Naked Lunch* and Arthur C. Clarke and Stanley Kubrick penned the screenplay of *2001: A Space Odyssey*. The Chelsea's more sensational reputation was established when Sid Vicious of the Sex Pistols killed his girlfriend Nancy here, and Andy Warhol used it for his movie, *The Chelsea Girls*.

East of Chelsea, at Broadway and 14th Street, is **Union Square**. In the mid-19th century, prominent families such as the Roosevelts lived in the surrounding streets. (You can visit the reconstruction of the **Theodore Roosevelt Birthplace** at East 20th Street ☎ 260-1616). Union Square was laid out as a park in 1831, and in the years before World War I it became a meeting place for political dissidents, socialists, and radicals. The annual Lesbian and Gay Pride Rally is held here in June.

Gramercy Park, located between East 20th and 21st Streets at Lexington Avenue, is the city's only remaining private park, open only to residents of the surrounding townhouses and apartment buildings. Built on the model of a London square, this exclusive neighborhood contains elegant 19th century buildings, two of which house **The Players Club** (founded in 1888 by Edwin Booth) and the **National Arts Club**.

At East 23rd Street and Fifth Avenue lies **Madison Square**. Here in 1845, a group of men codified the rules of American baseball forming the first American baseball team, the Knickerbocker Club. Take a moment to admire the **Flatiron Building**, which occupies the triangle made where Broadway meets Fifth

Avenue at 23rd Street. When it was erected in 1902, the 300 foot high structure caused quite a stir. New Yorkers ridiculed the oddly shaped edifice, predicting that it would crash down to the ground; instead it became the most frequently painted and photographed skyscraper of the era. It was originally named the Fuller Building, but everybody called it "Flatiron" because of its triangular shape, and the nickname stuck. A plethora of computer and multi-media companies have sprung up recently in the Flatiron district and the area is now often referred to as "Silicon Alley."

On the west side, in the blocks between 27th and 30th Streets on Avenue of the Americas (6th Avenue), you'll find New York's wholesale **Flower District**, which blooms at 4 o'clock in the morning when fresh flowers arrive from all parts of the country and from overseas. Remember to check out the weekend flea market on 6th Avenue (between 24th and 26th streets), a bargain hunters paradise, and cruisy to boot! (See Chapter 11.) The **Garment District**, which extends from 30th to 40th Streets on 6th and 7th Avenues, is crammed with wholesale distributors and specialty stores selling buttons, thread, and millinery. On the congested side streets you still see men pushing racks of clothing in between the traffic.

You cannot imagine a New York without the **Empire State Building**, located at 34th Street and 5th Avenue. The original Waldorf Astoria hotel was torn down to make way for the Art Deco edifice which has been part of the New York skyline since 1931, and which King Kong straddled in the movies. It remained the city's tallest building until the World Trade Center eclipsed it in 1976. Standing at 1,472 feet, the Empire State Building provides a marker by which you can orient yourself towards midtown. The lights at the top of the building are often colored for special holidays (lavender during Gay Pride Weekend); they are switched off at midnight. The observation decks on the 86th and 102nd floors are open to the public from 9:30 am to midnight (☎ 736-3100).

West of Empire State Building is **Herald Square**, where Broadway crosses 6th Avenue and 34th Street. It got its name from the now defunct *New York Herald* which had its offices nearby. Its main attraction, **Macy's** ("the world's largest store"), occupies an entire block.

Pennsylvania Station, one of New York's two major train stations (the other is Grand Central), is located a block west of Herald Square. The original Penn Station, an early 20th century architectural marvel from McKim, Mead & White, was wantonly torn down in the mid sixties. To add insult to injury, out of the ashes of the old station rose the latest incarnation of **Madison Square Garden**, a monstrous concrete drum-like structure, which many people hope will end up under a wrecker's ball as well. Now, under a new proposal, a new station may be built across the street on 8th Avenue in another McKim, Mead & White building, presently the **General Post Office**.

To many New Yorkers, the fate of the old Penn Station, a masterpiece of glass and steel, represents the downside of what Walt Whitman once called the city's tear-it-down-and-build-it-up-again spirit. A famous 1963 editorial in *The New York Times* noted, "we will probably be judged not by the monuments we build but by those we have destroyed". However, the destruction of Penn Station was the catalyst for establishing a New York City Landmarks Preservation Commission.

Moving east to 1st Avenue, visit the **United Nations Headquarters**, which was built in 1952 on an 18 acre site between 42nd & 48th Streets. The UN Secretariat, a 544-foot-high marble and glass slab, was New York's first glass tower, ☎ 963-7713 for details of guided tours. Nearby is **Turtle Bay Gardens**, two rows of houses along 48th and 49th Streets between 2nd and 3rd Avenues which share a common private garden; Katherine

Hepburn and Stephen Sondheim have townhouses here.

On East 42nd Street there are several buildings you should see. Although it is no longer the tallest, the **Chrysler Building,** at 405 Lexington Avenue, is one of the most eye-catching, and perhaps the most beloved skyscrapers in the New York skyline. Both during the day and at night (when it is specially lit) you can't miss the shiny stainless steel spire of this 1930 Art deco beauty. Built for the automobile company of the same name, all the decorative elements of the building are car-oriented: the gargoyles resemble hood ornaments and an abstract frieze of wheels with radiator caps encircles the building. Make sure you also check out the marble-adorned lobby.

The lobby of the **Chanin Building** at 122 East 42nd is another Art Deco wonder of marble and bronze. The interior of the **GreenPoint Bank** (110 East 42nd) is breath-taking; mosaic floors, limestone and sandstone walls and an imposing beamed ceiling give you the impression of a Romanesque palace.

Then there is the crown jewel of 42nd Street. Even if you don't have a train to catch visit **Grand Central Terminal**. Built between 1903-13, the Beaux Arts building is magnificent both inside and out. Floodlit at night, the entrance facing Park Avenue is adorned by a sculptural group representing Mercury, Hercules and Minerva and an ornate clock 13 feet in diameter. Inside, great arched windows allow sunlight to come flooding in, setting off the constellations of the zodiac which decorate the high vaulted ceiling. The information booth, topped by a four-faced brass clock, in the center of the main concourse is a good place to rendezvous with friends.

Travelling west from Grand Central, you'll find another opulent Beaux Arts edifice located on 5th Avenue between 40th and 42nd Streets. This is the Central Research Branch of the **New York Public Library** (☎ 661-7220). Two stone lions guard the entrance to the building, and marble staircases dominate the majestic hallway. There is no entrance fee, so go up to the Reading Room and feast your eyes on the architectural splendor of this 1911 building. **Bryant Park**, which was recently redesigned after years of neglect and occupancy by drug dealers, lies directly behind the library, and is a good place for an alfresco lunch in nice weather.

Westward lies the bright and glitzy, sometimes seedy **Times Square**. With its crowds and bright lights the intersection of Broadway and Seventh Avenue (the legendary "Crossroads of the World"), and the surrounding area (roughly 42nd to 48th Streets) has held a fascination for New Yorkers and visitors since the beginning of the century. Even today, the lighted signs, giant billboards, the motogram or "zipper" (which spells out news headlines in moving lights) draw millions of visitors from all over the world.

Originally called Longacre Square, a center for carriage shops and stables, its name and character changed when *The New York Times* moved its offices there on New Year's Eve, 1904. That event was celebrated with fireworks, a tradition which continues to this day. New Year's Eve at Times Square (when the famous lighted ball atop the former Times building is dropped at the stroke of midnight) is a raucous, crowded public event, that most sane people will gladly avoid.

At the turn of the century new theaters built on **42nd Street** near Times Square, turned the area into yet another location for New York's peripatetic **Theater District**, which spread into the neighboring blocks along Broadway. Theater and sex always seem to go hand in hand, and the city's redlight district gradually moved into Times Square and the nearby blocks of Eighth Avenue as well. Eventually the legitimate theaters on 42nd Street were converted to burlesque and movie houses, many of which in due course became (mostly straight) porn cinemas.

The Deuce, as the street was referred to by its underworld denizens, became a magnet for every sort, from the horny or curious tourist, the bible-thumping preacher and the prostitute to the drug dealer and petty thief.

But if you are looking for the sleaze, moral crusades or the demi-monde, chances are you won't find it in today's revitalized, tourist-oriented Times Square. In their place you will find theme restaurants, multiplex cinemas and the world's largest record superstore. The whole district is undergoing a significant makeover; new zoning laws have banished the sex establishments to the outskirts of Manhattan. Several of the derelict 42nd Street theaters are being restored to their former grandeur and the Walt Disney Company plans to open a major entertainment center and hotel in the area.

West of Times Square: The **Port Authority Bus Terminal**, the primary entry point to New York City via bus from the rest of the US, is located at the corner of 42nd Street and 8th Avenue. West of Eighth Avenue lies **Hell's Kitchen**. Once a neighborhood of slums, stables and slaughterhouses, the stomping ground for dangerous local Irish gangs in the early part of the 20th century, Hell's Kitchen has undergone considerable gentrification. Its polite name now is **Clinton** (after a former Governor, not the President), and it's home to many gay men — and to the many men and women who work in the nearby theater district. Walk west down 42nd Street to the Hudson River and you'll find Pier 83 from where the Circle Line begins its tour. Nearby, the **Intrepid Sea-Air-Space Museum** (☎ 245-2533), a museum of technology and naval history, is housed in an actual World War II aircraft carrier berthed at the pier.

Ninth Avenue is rather pleasant; it is famous for the many ethnic restaurants lining the way up to 57th Street. Several restaurants popular with the Broadway theatergoing crowd are clustered on **Restaurant Row**, 46th Street between 8th and 9th Avenues.

Before you leave the Times Square area pay a visit to the **Paramount Hotel** on West 46th (near 8th Avenue). It's a nice place to meet a friend for coffee. The lobby, designed by Philippe Starck, is full of delightful tongue-in-cheek surprises, and the male hotel staff is chosen with exquisite taste. Make it a point to visit the men's room, the campiest bathroom in New York!

Take a walk down 44th Street between 5th and 6th Avenues and stop by the famous **Algonquin Hotel**. This is the home of the legendary Round Table, the meeting place of the likes of Dorothy Parker, Alexander Woolcott and Robert Benchley. It was here that *The New Yorker* was born, and where Lerner and Loewe wrote *My Fair Lady*. And if that isn't pedigree enough, consider this: this was where Jacqueline Bisset picked up a hot young stud in George Cukor's last film, *Rich and Famous*. Across the street is the **Royalton Hotel**. It dates back to 1898, but it is worth visiting for the lobby. Resembling a futuristic ocean liner, this is another camp classic from Philippe Starck. Across the street is the **New York Yacht Club**, built in 1901, with windows designed to resemble the sterns of ships plowing through stormy waters.

No visit to New York is complete without a walk along **Fifth Avenue**, *The Avenue*. Still one of the more prestigious addresses in the city, it divides most of Manhattan into East and West and sometimes creates social, economic and geographic distinctions that only the native New Yorker understands. Fifth Avenue is Manhattan's ceremonial thoroughfare, the venue for most major city parades including the **Lesbian and Gay Pride Parade**.

In the late 19th century, the days of Edith Wharton's *The Age of Innocence*, most of the affluent families listed in New York's social register lived near 5th Avenue. Fashion changed as the blue bloods moved further north, and the midtown area of 5th Avenue, roughly between 50th and 59th Streets, became a prime retail store district, housing the most expensive stores in New York. The city bustles at Christmastime, and holiday shopping is a popular pastime for New Yorkers and out-of-towners alike; the Fifth Avenue stores are all decked out in glitter for the occasion.

Remember, nothing bad can ever happen to you at **Tiffany's**; window-shop at the famous store at 57th Street and have a coffee and Danish in memory of Audrey Hepburn. **St. Patrick's Cathedral**, an impressive gothic-style edifice, the seat of the Roman Catholic archdiocese of New York, and the Episcopalian **St. Thomas Church** are nearby.

Some of New York's most glamorous luxury hotels are also located in this vicinity. The **St. Regis-Sheraton Hotel** at 55th Street (built in 1904) is credited with being the birthplace of the Bloody Mary. At 59th Street stands the **Plaza Hotel**, built in 1907 to resemble a French Renaissance chateau; it boasts a magnificent view of Central Park. Truman Capote held his famous Black and White Ball here in 1966 and those who weren't invited left town rather than acknowledge they were left out. The Plaza is one of the most photogenic of New York hotels: Cary Grant got kidnapped from its lobby in *North by Northwest*, and more recently, in *Home Alone* 2, Macaulay Culkin asked for directions to the bathroom from Donald Trump, the Plaza's present owner.

Talking about Trump, one should mention the **Trump Tower**, a flashy, marble and bronze luxury shopping and apartment complex located on 5th Avenue between 56th and 57th Streets. If all the glitter and shine proves too much for you, walk around the corner to Madison and 55th Street where the monumental **Sony Building**, a quintessential post-modern work by gay architect Philip Johnson, provides a welcome contrast. Next door is the glass **IBM Building**. The two buildings provide free public spaces, ideal rest stops when trekking through Manhattan.

Take advantage of Manhattan's several vest-pocket parks,

welcome oases of green in the crowded metropolis. **Paley Park,** located off 5th Avenue on East 53rd Street, is a small, tranquil space with green trees, ivy and a waterfall designed to mute the sounds of nearby traffic. **Greenacre Park**, a bigger and even more beautiful pocket park is located on East 51st Street between 2nd and 3rd Avenues.

One of Midtown's biggest attractions is **Rockefeller Center**. Stretching from West 48th to 51st Streets between 5th and 6th Avenues, it was built principally between 1931 and 1940. A complex of 19 commercial buildings and a maze of underground passageways for pedestrians, it is a majestic example of Art Deco grandeur, perhaps the crowning glory of New York urban architectural development. Rockefeller Center buildings include **Radio City Music Hall** and the imposing 70-story **GE Building,** home to NBC studios and the famous Art Moderne restaurant, **The Rainbow Room**, on the 65th floor. In front of

ROCKEFELLER CENTER photo copyright © Stephen DiMenna

30 Rockefeller Plaza is a skating rink, which is converted into a restaurant from May through September. In December, the city kicks off the holiday season with the lighting of a giant Christmas tree installed on the sidewalk behind the rink.

The Museum of Modern Art is located on West 53rd Street between 5th and 6th Avenues and **Carnegie Hall** on 57th Street and 7th Avenue. Talk nicely to the doorman at **The Osborne** (diagonally across from Carnegie Hall) and he may let you peek into the sumptuous Tiffany-designed lobby of this 100-year-old apartment building. Also check out **Alwyn Court**, at 7th Avenue and 58th Street, an ornately decorated apartment building dating from 1909.

In the East Midtown area you might check out the prestigious **Waldorf Astoria Hotel** (Park Avenue between 49th and 50th Streets),which was built in 1931. The roster of celebrities who, over the years, have made the adjoining Waldorf Towers their temporary home include the Duke and Duchess of Windsor, Albert Einstein, Marilyn Monroe, President John F. Kennedy, Frank Sinatra and several international heads of state. A piano that once belonged to Cole Porter, another celebrated Waldorf resident, is installed in the lounge of Peacock Alley, the restaurant across from the main lobby.

The **Villard Houses**, on Madison Avenue and 50th Street, were designed by McKim, Mead & White. Five brownstone mansions were built in 1886 to resemble a Renaissance palazzo for the Austrian railroad baron Henry Villard. Today you'll see what's left of them preserved in the premises of the **New York Palace Hotel**. Stop by for afternoon tea at the fabulous Gold Room. Tennessee Williams met with his unfortunate death at the **Hotel Elysée** at East 54th Street (near Park Avenue). Williams nicknamed it "Hotel Easy-Lay" because of its close proximity to the hustlers of East 53rd Street. The management does not welcome visitors asking to see where the great playwright died, and in any event his rooms, the appropriately titled Sunset Suite, have since been demolished.

In the same vicinity, pay a visit to **St. Bartholomew's Church** on Park Avenue between 50th and 51st Streets, admire its unique dome, and check out the former **General Electric Building/ RCA Victor Building** at Lexington Avenue and 51st Street. This tower, built in 1931, was specially designed to blend with the Byzantine lines of the church. Notice the spiky crown of the building is composed of abstract lightning bolts in honor of its original tenant, the Radio Company of America (RCA). The building now belongs to Columbia University. On the west side of Lexington Avenue just south of 52nd Street, you will pass over the subway grating from which a gust of air blew Marilyn Monroe's skirts in *The Seven Year Itch*. The **Citicorp Center**, a 1978 office complex across the street, stands out against the New York skyline with its aluminum-covered top slanted at 45 degrees. There is a large public atrium in this building surrounded by numerous shops and restaurants; free public concerts are often held here. **St. Peter's Church**, the "jazz church" is located in the Citicorp complex. The onion-domed **Central Synagogue** (built in 1872) is located across Lexington Avenue at 55th Street.

A mere 300 yards off the east shore of Manhattan near 59th Street lies **Roosevelt Island**. You may want to spend an afternoon here. Though only three and a half minutes away by cable car, the ride is spectacular and it's so quiet and peaceful that, despite the fact that it is a thriving urban community, it feels more like a remote village. The tramway station is located on 2nd Avenue between 59th and 60th Streets, right next to the imposing Queensboro Bridge.

UPTOWN
(Above 59th Street)

Upper East Side

The Upper East Side is a large area encompassing several neighborhoods, but it is best known for its block after block of elegant luxury apartment houses which line Fifth and Park Avenues. The stretch between 70th and 90th Streets, where wealthy families like the Carnegies, Astors, Pulitzers and Whitneys built themselves magnificent houses, was once called Millionaire's Row; the few remaining mansions have been converted to museums, foreign consulates, private schools, clubs and the like. The heavy-hitting cultural institutions on Fifth between 83rd and 103rd Streets have dubbed this stretch of the avenue **Museum Mile**. It's a veritable smorgasbord of culture. We are talking of the **Metropolitan Museum of Art**, the **Guggenheim Museum**, **The National Academy of Design**, the **Cooper-Hewitt Museum**, **The Jewish Museum**, **The International Center of Photography**, **The Museum of the City of New York** and **El Museo Del Barrio**. **Madison Avenue**, one block east, is an unbroken string of art galleries, antique shops, expensive boutiques and fancy eateries up to 86th Street. In spite of its finery, the Upper East Side can also be rather dull; it's certainly not as vibrant as the gayer sections of the city.

Yorkville, centered around East 86th Street was a small 18th century hamlet which became home to waves of German immigrants in the early part of this century. Similar enclaves of Czechs and Hungarians settled in the neighboring East 70s.

Take a walk along the promenade in **Carl Schurz Park** (East End Avenue between 84th and 90th Streets). You get a superb view of the East River and three Manhattan bridges from here. Situated at the north end of the park is the elegant

Gracie Mansion, the official residence of the Mayor of New York, which was built 1799 as a country home for a Scottish merchant, ☎ 570-4751 for details about tours.

Above 96th Street and east of Madison Avenue lies **East Harlem** or **Spanish Harlem**, the cradle of Latin American culture in New York. The mostly Puerto Rican residents call the area **El Barrio** ("the neighborhood"). The commercial center of the Barrio is **La Marquetta**, an enclosed market located between 110th and 116th Streets under the railway tracks on Park Avenue.

Central Park

However short your visit to New York, find time for **Central Park**. New Yorkers from all walks of life enjoy the varied pleasures of this magnificent public patch of green, known as the lungs of the city. You'll see why they are immensely proud of this entirely man-made, 843-acre landscape designed by Frederick Law Olmsted and Calvert Vaux. Work was begun in 1857 in what was then a swamp, occupied by squatters and primarily used as a garbage dump. When the principal work was completed 16 years later, the park became a potpourri of varied lakes, meadows, wooded areas, and gardens supporting hundreds of species of trees and shrubs, and a large population of birds.

Many gay men sunbathe on **Sheep's Meadow** (67th-70th Streets by the West Drive); sheep did actually graze here once. You get a marvelous view of the Midtown skyscrapers from the hill near the meadow. **Strawberry Fields**, a peaceful grove near West 72nd Street, is Yoko Ono's memorial to John Lennon, who lived in the Dakota apartment house across the street. The densely wooded **Ramble** (74th-79th Streets between East and West Drives) is a haven for bird watchers and a notoriously cruisy spot for gay men. You can rent boats and bicycles at the **Loeb Boathouse**, skate at the **Wollman Rink**, jog around **The Jacqueline Kennedy Onassis Reservoir** and go riding on a horse rented from the **Claremont Stables**.

Climb up to the top of **Belvedere Castle** (79th Street at West Drive), a scaled down version of a Scottish stronghold, and you'll get a superlative view of the entire park. The **Shakespeare Garden** nearby is planted with trees and plants mentioned in the works of the Bard. **The Delacorte Theater** (80th Street at the West Drive) is home to the New York Shakespeare Festival's free Shakespeare in the Park summer season. **Central Park Zoo** at 64th Street and Fifth Avenue, which was renovated in 1988, contains 450 animals representing about 100 different species (☎ 861-6030). Record crowds have flocked to the 15-acre **Great Lawn** between 80th and 85th Streets to hear Diana Ross, Elton John, Simon & Garfunkel and Luciano Pavarotti perform, to hear Pope John Paul II say mass, and to attend the annual summer performances from the New York Philharmonic and Metropolitan Opera. The so-called **Cleopatra's Needle** obelisk (82nd Street at East Drive) was actually built by King Thotmes III in 1600 BC. Its twin stands on the bank of the Thames in London. Finally, pay a visit to the **Conservatory Garden**, a hidden gem near 105th Street and 5th Avenue. The entrance to these three formal gardens is marked by an iron gate which was once part of Cornelius Vanderbilt II's mansion.

The Park is generally safe during daylight hours. Be alert, however, after dark and in secluded wooded areas. You can get maps and other information for Central Park at the Visitor Center located at 65th Street and 5th Avenue, ☎ 794-6564.

Upper West Side

The Upper West Side was populated in the early part of the 20th century principally by Eastern European Jews from the

Lower East Side. It did not have the same social cachet as the Upper East Side, where the elite families maintained luxurious mansions, but it has always had a liberal, intellectual and artistic reputation.

A focal point of the city's creative energies is the **Lincoln Center**, the country's premier performing arts complex which occupies 14 acres on West 62nd to 66th Streets, between Columbus and Amsterdam Avenues. Before construction commenced on the center in 1959, this area was a low-income tenement district, and served as a movie set for the opening shots of *West Side Story*. The six-building complex is currently home to the Metropolitan Opera, New York City Opera, New York City Ballet, the Lincoln Center Theater, the Chamber Music Society, and the Film Society. It is also the site of the Performing Arts Branch of the New York Public Library, Juillard School, the School of American Ballet and the City Center of Music and Drama.

Though much of the Upper West Side is occupied by middle-class housing, the area is also known for its spacious brownstone houses and some striking luxury apartment buildings. Take a look at the following: **Hotel des Artistes** (67th Street and Central Park West), a 1913 studio complex originally built for artists. Isadora Duncan and Noel Coward lived here once; it is now an expensive co-op with the four-star **Cafe des Artistes** located on the ground floor. The **Dakota**, a 1884 luxury apartment house which served as the eerie location for *Rosemary's Baby*, is located on West 72nd and Central Park West. The Dakota has been home to Leonard Bernstein, Rudolf Nureyev, Lauren Bacall, and John Lennon, who was assassinated in front of the building in 1980. The **Ansonia Hotel**, built in 1904 on Broadway between 73rd and 74th Streets, is an elaborately decorated grand Belle Epoque masterpiece with rounded towers. The home of many prominent musicians including Enrico Caruso,

Igor Stravinsky, Ezio Pinza and Arturo Toscanini, it recently served as a gothic setting for the thriller *Single White Female*. The famous Continental Baths, one of the best known New York gay bathhouses, was located in this building, and it was here that the gay community, and subsequently the rest of the world, discovered the divine Bette Midler.

The Upper West Side waterfront is spectacular, particularly near **Riverside Park** (from West 72nd Street). The park was planned by Olmsted, architect of Central Park, and its promenade along the Hudson is a favorite with cyclists and lovers. The **79th Street Boat Basin** (entrance in the park) is home to a few New Yorkers who actually live in houseboats. Along **Riverside Drive** (also laid out by Olmsted) you will see many fine examples of New York brownstones. Between 105th and 106th Streets, you will see some of the best turn-of-the-century French Beaux Arts townhouses in the area.

Morningside Heights

The primary landmarks in this hilly ridge of upper Manhattan (bounded by Cathedral Parkway and 125th Street) are the **Cathedral of St. John the Divine, Riverside Church, Grant's Tomb** and **Columbia University**. When completed, St. John the Divine (112th Street and Amsterdam Avenue) will be the largest Gothic-style cathedral in the world. The structure was begun in 1892 and may take another 70 years to finish. Its nave, which can seat 5,000 worshippers, is the size of two American football fields. Riverside Church (120th Street and Riverside Drive) is one of the most progressive churches in the country. It was built in 1930, using the cathedral of Chartres in France as a model. Visit the observation platform at the top of the church tower (open Sundays 12:30pm-3:30pm). Grant's Tomb, located near Riverside Church at 122nd Street, contains the remains of Civil

War General and U.S. President, Ulysses S. Grant, and his wife. The massive granite mausoleum was inspired by Napoleon's tomb at the Hôtel des Invalides in Paris. Columbia University's main campus lies along Broadway between 114th and 120th Streets. Originally Kings College, Columbia was chartered in Lower Manhattan in 1754. The school moved to its present location in 1897 and is the center of a highly renowned academic community located along Broadway: **Barnard College** (117th Street); **Teacher's College** (120th Street); **Union Theological Seminary** (121st Street); **Jewish Theological Seminary** (122nd Street) and **Manhattan School of Music** (122nd Street). A special attraction of this most tranquil of New York neighborhoods is, of course, the boys of Columbia. Boywatchers are known to grab any excuse to visit the main quadrangle of the Columbia campus, especially in the summer when skimpily clad students sun themselves on the steps of the imposing Low Library building.

Harlem

Don't let exaggerated rumors of crime and violence deter you from exploring one of New York's important neighborhoods. Harlem *is* the soul of New York's Black community and, at one point in time, represented the apogee of African-American culture. Like anywhere else in the city, parts of Harlem are economically depressed and are to be avoided, but the neighborhood's famous sights are easily accessible and near main thoroughfares. You will find the **Harlem Visitors and Convention Association** (☎ 427-3317) a useful source of information and advice on these matters.

The Dutch established a northern outpost in what was originally an Indian village in 1658, and called it Nieuw Haarlem. The settlement was connected to New Amsterdam, ten miles to the south, by a road (now part of Broadway) built by Black slaves.

Harlem remained remote farmland until the opening of the New York and Harlem River Railroad in 1837, whereupon many well-to-do families moved north. Jews and Blacks began to move into the area in the early 20th century, following the building of the subways and the subsequent increase in real estate development. The 1920's witnessed the Harlem Renaissance, a remarkable flowering of Black culture in jazz, poetry, literature and art which made Harlem world famous. The 1960s struggle for Black civil rights was fought, in part, out of Harlem. Today, as Harlem shows signs of renewing itself economically, it may be the next Manhattan neighborhood due for gentrification.

Harlem has some of the city's finest brownstone townhouses. Pay a visit to **'Striver's Row'** in the **St. Nicholas Historical District** (137th to 139th Streets between Adam Clayton Powell, Jr., and Frederick Douglass Boulevards). The four rows of handsome dwellings, built in 1891, got this nickname from the young ambitious professionals who lived there. The **Mt. Morris Historic District** (120th to 124th Streets between Adam Clayton Powell, Jr., Boulevard and Madison Avenue) includes a particularly elegant set of brownstones dating back to the early 1880s. Residents in this district open their houses to visitors one week every June, ☎ 289-7051 for details. The adjoining Marcus Garvey Memorial Park unfortunately is not well maintained.

In the **Jumel Historic District** (Edgecome Avenue at West 160th Street) you will find well-preserved 19th century row houses and the **Morris-Jumel Mansion**, which, dating back to 1765, is one of the city's few remaining pre-Revolutionary buildings. At Convent Avenue and 141st Street, squashed behind a church, stands the **Hamilton Grange**, home of Alexander Hamilton, first Secretary of the Treasury (☎ 283-5154). The area called the **Hamilton Heights Historic District** was once part of his country estate in the early 19th century. **Sugar Hill** is the name for the section of the heights between St. Nicholas and Edgecome

Avenues around 143rd Street. Many prominent Black figures, including Duke Ellington, Count Basie and the former Supreme Court Justice Thurgood Marshall lived here. This district also has a superb collection of decorative row houses dating from the turn of the century; the district's homeowner's association provide house tours during a week in June, ☎ 283-5154.

Harlem was dubbed the "Home of Churches" by the celebrated poet Langston Hughes. Its most influential church, both spiritually and politically, is the **Abyssinian Baptist Church** (138th Street between Malcolm X & Adam Clayton Powell, Jr. Boulevards). The **United Baptist Church** (145th Street between Adam Clayton Powell, Jr. and Frederick Douglaas Boulevards) and **Child's Memorial Temple** (Amsterdam between 147th and 148th Streets) are renowned for their gospel choirs. Other important Harlem churches are **Mt. Olivet Baptist Church** (Malcolm X Boulevard and West 120th Street), which was built as a synagogue in 1907, and **St. Martin's Church** (Malcolm X Boulevard and West 122nd Street), an 1888 Romanesque Episcopal church famous for its stained glass mosaics and a majestic carillon. At 116th Street and Lenox Avenue you'll find the **Malcolm Shabazz Mosque**, a former casino which was converted into a mosque in the 1960s. It's named after Malcom X, who once preached there.

Harlem's most famous cultural landmark is the **Apollo Theater** (125th Street, between 7th & 8th Avenues). The collection of the **Schomburg Center for Research in Black Culture** (Malcolm X Boulevard at 135th Street), a branch of the New York Public Library, is said to be the finest in the United States on the history and literature of the African diaspora (☎ 491-2200). The **Studio Museum of Harlem** is a repository for the work of African-American, Caribbean-American and Hispanic-American artists, and the **Black Fashion Museum** has a unique collection tracing the history of Black design.

Harlem's biggest festival is **Harlem Week**, celebrated over a two week period from the first Monday through the third Sunday in August. The best that Harlem has to offer is showcased for visitors from all over the world, ☎ 427-3315 for information.

Washington Heights and Inwood

The Cloisters, the medieval branch of the Metropolitan Museum of Art, is situated near the northern tip of Manhattan in beautiful **Fort Tryon Park** (West 190th and Dyckman Streets), which was landscaped by Frederick Law Olmsted, Jr., son of the Central Park architect. The views of the Hudson River from this vantage point and the serenity of The Cloisters are well worth the trip uptown. Manhattan's last surviving Dutch colonial farmhouse, the **Dyckman House**, is located at the corner of West 204th Street and Broadway. It is now restored as a museum and provides a fascinating insight into farmlife during the colonial era. ☎ 304-9422.

Finally, if you want to see what Manhattan might have looked like before the arrival of the Europeans, visit **Inwood Hill Park** near 214th Street. The only remaining wilderness in Manhattan, it reveals a fascinating geological profile of the island. Here, for example, you will see ridges of the volcanic bedrock, Manhattan Schist (only sparsely seen above ground in Central Park), and exposures of Inwood Marble. Inwood Hill Park was the last refuge of the native tribes as they were pushed back by the European colonists.

Books

As you see it is impossible in one chapter to cover everything of interest in Manhattan; entire books have been written about single neighborhoods. I recommend the following books if you want to learn more about New York: *Blue Guide New York*; the *Access Guide to New York City*; *New Yorkwalks* (The 92nd Street Y); *AIA Guide to New York City* (American Institute of Architects); *Insight Guide to New York*, *Guide to New York City Landmarks* (NY Landmarks Presentation Committee), *A City Observed: A Guide to the Architecture of Manhattan* by Paul Goldberger, and the recently published *Encyclopedia of New York* edited by Kenneth T. Jackson.

Tours

The New York Convention and Visitors Bureau (☎ 484-1200) provides a brochure listing all the tours available in New York. Here are a few worth considering:

Circle Line: Departs from Pier 83 (West 42nd Street at the Hudson River). Duration 3 hours, $18. ☎ 563-3200

Harlem Your Way Tours ☎ 609 1196

New York Double Decker bus tours, $15. ☎ 967-6008

Liberty Helicopter Tours from $55 to $119 per person. ☎ 465-8905

Shoestring Safaris $5. ☎ 265-2663

The Municipal Art Society conducts architectural, historical, social and cultural tours and walks of New York City $10-15 per walk. ☎ 439-1049 or 935-3960 for information.

92nd Street Y Tours unique walking and bus tours throughout New York City. ☎ 996-1100

Urban Park Rangers conduct excellent free tours in all five boroughs. ☎ 427-4040

6: A BRIEF HISTORY OF GAY NEW YORK

by Franklin Headley

Cities have always been hubs for lusty men and boys to act on their sexual impulses with a degree of anonymity impossible in country towns. For this reason, New York City from its founding, but particularly from the beginning of the nineteenth century, grew to be an erotic mecca for soldier, sailor, merchant, immigrant and tourist alike.

Cruising grounds of nineteenth-century Manhattan differed little from those of today: public toilets, parks, and the occasional private club. In addition, churches were popular for trysts since they were usually dark and unlocked. Walt Whitman enjoyed watching Brooklyn youths swim naked in the East River. Horatio Alger, the novelist who wrote rag-to-riches stories of young boys in such popular works as *Ragged Dick* and *Tattered Tom*, found his own treasures by hanging around the Newsboy Lodging House. His favorite was a ten-year-old Chinese boy named Wing. Before Central Park's Ramble was laid out, one also could pick up a trick at City Hall Park and Cedar Street. Around lower Broadway and the Bowery, male hustlers wore red bowties to announce their profession to interested passers by. They would occasionally catch the eye of a straight guy. As the historian George Chauncey, Jr. has argued, heterosexuals felt much less inhibited to do the deed with other men since they believed themselves to be so highly sexed even women could not completely satisfy them.

The Village became in the early twentieth century a community where homosexuals could find and help create their own public spaces. Known then as the remote Ninth Ward, the Village was inhabited mainly by Italian immigrants. Within a few years, however, the bohemians arrived and rechristened the area with its colonial name, Greenwich Village. The area's gay character emerged soon after, since homosexuals could clothe themselves in the garb of bohemianism while living out their lifestyles. Before 1920 there was a song written which included the line, "Fairyland's not far from Washington Square". The IRT subway completed along Seventh Avenue in 1917 and IND along Sixth in 1927-1930 encouraged queers to flock to this often more tolerant part of the city. Gay and lesbian tearooms multiplied during this time. On the east side of town, the first Village balls were held at Webster Hall on Eleventh Street and Third Avenue. Gay life in Harlem became an uptown extension of the Village and was a queen's paradise, where drag balls were held at the Rockland Palace and the Savoy Ballroom. At Harlem speakeasies, patrons could enjoy lesbian performers such as Bessie Smith and Ma Rainey.

Prohibition (1920-1933) helped to transform an emerging gay bar culture into an underground network of speakeasies and helped to forge gay bars' long-term relationship with organized crime. The 1930's saw the creation of the first gay resort, Cherry Grove on Fire Island. Automats in the Tenderloin region (the area in Midtown including Times Square) were alternative locales for straight-acting and often middle-class gays to meet and socialize. The more flamboyant and proletarian queens dominated areas like Bryant Park, behind the New York Public Library.

After World War II brought more single guys to New York, gay life became even more conspicuous. For the gay tourist in the know, the entire city seemed centered around gay entertainments. Many bars and restaurants were at certain times of the day gayer than others. Gay spaces also became highly specialized. By the 1960s, the Oak Room at the Plaza Hotel was considered "high drag". Meticulously feminine drag queen patrons were often upstaged here by the more flamboyant real female customers whose heavy make-up and elaborate hair-dos often caused them to be mistaken for impersonators. "Low drag" queens, whom no one would confuse with women, stuck to neighborhood bars.

The Sixty-third Street YMCA on the west side was considered the capitol of the New York gay world. A popular spot for vertical action was the standing-room-only back row of the old Metropolitan Opera House at 39th and Broadway. Kelly's bar on 45th Street was the place to find that adorable hustler. Cruising in public toilets proliferated, especially since many subway and el stations had johns, and the ambitious queer could do every station on the west side in a single evening. Central Park was then as much an alluring and occasionally deadly attraction at night as it is today. But during the day birdwatchers and cruisers happily commingled. The porn theaters of the 70s and 80s around 42nd Street and Eighth Avenue were once popular movie houses, but often served the same purposes. One only needed to stick to the balconies.

Of course, in any of these places, there was the constant threat of violence and harassment by the police. Gay bars continued a close relationship with organized crime because without such protection they could not have anticipated or survived police raids. The Stonewall Rebellion in 1969 finally demanded, above all, the legitimacy of gay space in New York City. Even before Stonewall, however, gay life in the City became increasingly politicized. The Mattachine Society established a chapter here in 1955 and the first gay student organization was founded at Columbia University in 1966. After Stonewall a series of organizations tried to galvanize gay New Yorkers from the new left Gay Liberation Front to the Gay Activist Alliance, the main proponent of the lambda symbol. The AIDS crisis radically transformed gay organizations and politics. The playwright and activitist Larry Kramer co-founded the Gay Men's Health Crisis (GMHC) in 1981 and then founded the more politically proactive AIDS Coalition To Unleash Power (ACT UP) in 1987. New York City passed a gay rights bill in 1986, but similar legislation for New York State has still to get through a conservative majority.

The AIDS crisis led to the gradual closing of bathhouses and backrooms. By the mid-80s, promiscuous public sex in New York City was probably at an all time low. The 90s has seen public sex become much more fashionable with the reopening of backrooms throughout the city (although the pendulum seems to be swinging back now that there's a Republican major in office.) But there are now countless ways to meet, from phone sex lines advertised on public access television to the Gay Pride Parade commemorating Stonewall every June. Gotham gaiety has never been more public.

The sources for this essay provide a good starting point for further reading. The best overall source is George Chauncey Jr.'s *Gay New York: 1890-1940*. Of more general interest are the entries relating to New York in *The Encyclopedia of Homosexuality*, edited by Wayne Dynes.

7: GAY NEW YORK
PUBLICATIONS & ORGANIZATIONS

NEW YORK GAY PUBLICATIONS

CHRISTOPHER STREET
P.O. Box 1475, Church Street Station, New York, NY 10008
☎ 627-2120
Monthly Gay literary magazine launched in 1976. Over the years it has featured writers such as Edmund White, John Preston and Andrew Holleran and, currently, Quentin Crisp.

HX MAGAZINE
19 West 21st Street
New York, NY 10010
☎ 627-0747; Fax: 627-5280
Website: http://www.hx.com
Weekly. Launched in 1991 as *Homo Xtra*, this gossipy, pocket sized magazine is your best resource for up-to-date information on bars, clubs, restaurants, entertainment and the nightlife scene. You can pick it up free at most bars, clubs and gay bookstores, or buy it at newsstands and magazine stores.

LESBIAN AND GAY NEW YORK (LGNY)
225 Lafayette Street, Suite 1103
New York, NY 10012
☎ 343-7200; Fax: 343-9327
Website: http:/www.gravity.fly.net
Weekly newspaper. Since its launch in 1994, *LGNY* has emerged as New York's premier gay and lesbian newspaper and provides good coverage of the local gay political scene.

METROSOURCE
496A Hudson Street, D 12
New York, NY 10014
☎ 691-5127; Fax: 741-2978
Quarterly. Distributed at bars and gay establishments. *Metrosource* contains bar listings, restaurant notes, feature articles, travel stories as well as a gay business and organization directory.

NEW YORK NATIVE
P.O. Box 1475, Church Street Station, New York, NY 10008
☎ 627-2120; Fax: 727-9321
Weekly. Started in 1980 by the publisher of *Christopher Street, The Native* was the first publication in the country to alert the community to the spread of AIDS. The newspaper has since pursued a controversial editorial policy challenging

theories and assumptions endorsed by the medical establishment and the gay community at large with regard to AIDS.

NEXT
121 Varrick Street, 3rd Floor
New York, NY 10013
☎ 627-0165; Fax 627-0633
Weekly. A sleek, colorized answer to *HX* which also provides bar, club and restaurant guides, and information about current events. Available free at bars and gay establishments.

OUT
110 Greene Street, Suite 800
New York, NY 10012
☎ 334-9119; Fax: 334-9227
Subscriptions: P.O Box 15307, North Hollywood, California 91615,
☎ (800) 876-1199
Website: http://www.out.com
Publishes 10 issues per year. A glossy, general interest magazine for gay men and lesbians, *Out* is the indisputed leader among the gay and lesbian magazines published in the U.S.

POZ
349 West 12th Street
New York, NY 10014
☎ 242-2163; Fax: 675-8505
Subscriptions: ☎ (800) 883-2163
Monthly glossy magazine with features and information aimed at HIV+ people.

• The following California based publications are also available in New York:

THE ADVOCATE
Bi weekly with a strong national profile. One of the oldest gay publications in the country, it contains news stories, interviews, features and reviews of interest to lesbians and gay men. *The Advocate*'s Classified section containing sex ads, advice and erotic fiction is published separately.

GENRE
Monthly lifestyle magazine for gay men, which promotes itself as a gay version of *Esquire* and *GQ*.

• Skin magazines (mostly California based), usually featuring porn stars and photos from their movies, are available by subscription as well as at bookstores. Unlike in other American cities, you can buy most porno mags at street-corner newsstands. Popular titles include: *Fresh Men*; *In Touch*; *Mandate*; *Drummer*; *Playguy*; *Inches*; *Torso* and *Honcho*. For erotic fiction pick up such titles as *First Hand*; *Guys* and *Manscape*.

GAY INTERNET

GAY GUIDE NEW YORK
http://www.gayguidenewyork.com

NEW YORK CYBERQUEERS (NYCQ)
Email: NYCQ@NYCNET.com
Website: http://www.NYCQ.org

QUEER RESOURCES DIRECTORY
http://www.qrd.org

NYC NET
http://www.nycnet.com
email: info@nycnet.com
☎ 268-9285
New York's premier gay and lesbian on-line service. Digitally connecting New York's queer community, NYC NET offers a plethora of services: queer forums, a directory for gay and lesbian organizations, an NYC calendar of events, *Genre* and *Vice* magazines on-line, several chat groups and internet queer newsgroups, etc.

GAY ORGANIZATIONS

The following is a selection from the innumerable gay groups and organizations in New York that reflect the great diversity and varied interests of our community. Groups relating to culture and sport may be found in the chapters relating to those subjects.

• In all the listings that follow, "The Center" refers to the Lesbian and Gay Community Services Center, 208 West 13th Street. All telephone numbers are in the (212) area code unless otherwise indicated.

THE LESBIAN & GAY COMMUNITY SERVICES CENTER
208 West 13th Street (7th & 8th Avenues)
New York, NY 10011
☎ 620-7310; Fax: 924-2657
Website: http://www.panix.com/~dhuppert/gay/center
Open seven days a week, 9:00am to 11:00pm.

Founded in 1983, The Center can justifiably claim to provide the "political, cultural, spiritual and emotional sustenance" of the gay community. More than 400 groups rent space at The Center for meetings, social events and cultural programs. Its current building, a former high school erected in 1842, shows its age but has a certain homespun charm. The Center plans a multi-million dollar renovation and expansion as soon as it raises the funds. The Center is a good place to get oriented in gay New York; information about the gay community, as well as many local publications are available free of charge here. Unlike similar institutions elsewhere in the world, the Center currently lacks a cafeteria, but it's surrounded by the countless

KEITH HARING MURAL photo courtesey of The Center

bars and restaurants of Greenwich Village.

The Center houses the National Museum & Archive of Lesbian and Gay History. Launched in 1989, it was the first museum of its kind in the United States. Open Thursdays at 8:00pm (or by appointment with Center Archivist Rich Wandel). Various site-specific artworks were commissioned by the Center Museum for Stonewall's 20th anniversary and remain in the building permanently. When you visit the Center take a look at the gloriously priapic Keith Haring mural in the men's room on the second floor.

The Pat Parker & Vito Russo Center Library (open Mondays and Wednesdays 6:00pm-8:00pm and Saturdays 1:00pm-4:00pm), a joint project with The Publishing Triangle (a gay publishing organization), makes gay and lesbian literature available to the community. The Community Health Project (See Chapter 9), and the Coalition for Lesbian and Gay Rights, ☎ 627 1398, also have offices at the Center.

The Center operates Orientation, a monthly "welcome wagon" to introduce newcomers to New York's gay and lesbian community, and a number of other programs including: Project Connect, an Alcohol & Drug intervention program; CenterBridge, AIDS related bereavement services; Gender Identity Project, information, referrals and peer counseling for gender conflicted groups — male to female and female to male support groups; Center Youth Enrichment Services, creative arts workshops for lesbians and gay men under 20 years of age; In Our Own Write, readings by emerging writers and workshops to foster new talent, and Center Dances on Saturdays 9:00pm-1:00am.

Call The Center for a complete listing of its programs and events.

COMMUNITY SERVICES

GAY AND LESBIAN SWITCHBOARD OF NEW YORK

648 Broadway, Suite 402
New York, NY 10012
☎ 777-1800 (10:30am to midnight daily)

A telephone service operated by gay and lesbian volunteers. Founded in 1974, GLSB is an invaluable "information central" for the community referring callers to gay owned businesses, doctors and lawyers, political organizations, neighborhood groups, AIDS service organizations and religious and sports groups, and providing information about bars, clubs and restaurants. Call also if you need a "friendly listener" and counselor to whom you can talk in confidence about issues relating to coming out, AIDS anxiety, depression and trouble with relationships.

HERITAGE OF PRIDE

154 Christopher Street
New York, NY 10014
☎ 807-7433; Fax : 807-7436

A non profit, volunteer group which organizes the various events for the Gay/Lesbian Pride held in the last weekend of June. (See Chapter 4)

THE HETRICK MARTIN INSTITUTE (HMI)

2 Astor Place
New York, NY 10003
☎ 674-2400

A not for profit social service organization for lesbian and gay adolescents, founded in 1979. Services include counseling, health advocacy and street outreach to homeless teenagers. HMI also operates the Harvey Milk School, a high school for gay, lesbian and bisexual youth, established in 1985.

NYC GAY & LESBIAN ANTI-VIOLENCE PROJECT

647 Hudson Street
New York, NY 10014
☎ 807-6761
24 hour hotline: ☎ 807-0197

An organization which provides counseling, advocacy and information for survivors of anti-gay and anti-lesbian violence, sexual assault, HIV related violence, domestic violence and other types of criminal victimization. NGLAV keeps track of all reported acts of violence against gay men and lesbians.

AIDS/HIV

ACT UP (AIDS Coalition to Unleash Power) NEW YORK

332 Bleecker Street, Suite G5
New York, NY 10014
☎ 642-5499; Fax: 366-4909
Email: ACTUPNY@panix.com

A diverse, non partisan, group "united in anger and committed to direct-action to end the AIDS crisis," founded in 1987 by activist/ writer Larry Kramer. ACT UP has various committees, caucuses and working groups addressing all aspects of the AIDS Crisis. In the fight against AIDS and the bureaucracy that allowed the disease to become a national disaster, ACT UP can claim several major victories. As a result of its activism the federal drug approval process was revolutionized; New York City has attempted (in less conservative times) to adopt more aggressive AIDS prevention measures such as distributing condoms in schools and instituting a clean needle exchange programs; and drug manufacturers have brought down their prices. ACT UP's protests and demonstrations, sit ins and "die ins", "phone zaps," "fax zaps" and "mail zaps" targeting politicians and drug companies, serve as models for current civil disobedience and activism. The slogans, "ACT UP! FIGHT BACK! FIGHT AIDS!" and "SILENCE=DEATH" are known all over the world. ACT UP also produced a whole new look in the gay community: young, active, aggressive, militant, and, let's face it, sexy. The group meets every Monday at 7:30pm. at The Center.

AIDS MEMORIAL IN THE VILLAGE

P.O. Box 843, Village Station
New York, NY 10014
☎ (718) 565-6789

A permanent memorial established in June 1992 to honor everybody who has died of AIDS or contracted the virus since 1981. An eternal flame and individually engraved name plates are located in the first balcony of St. Veronica's Church, 149 Christopher Street, open to visitors daily.

AIDS PREVENTION ACTION LEAGUE (APAL)

349 West 12th Street
New York, NY 10014
☎ 229-9102

An AIDS activist group that aims to prevent the disease through direct action, advocacy and education. APAL, which meets at the Center on Thursday evenings, has been in the forefront of the drive to keep sex clubs and venues open but safe in New York City.

DAY WITHOUT ART, TIMES SQUARE photo copyright Tina Pau

AIDS TREATMENT DATA NETWORK

259 West 30th Street, 9th Floor
New York, NY 10001
☎ 268-4196; Fax 268-4199;
Spanish language ☎ (800) 858-2111;
Provides information on HIV treatments and experimental drugs, and support services for people with HIV their lovers and medical care providers.

AMERICAN FOUNDATION FOR AIDS RESEARCH

733 Third Avenue, 12th Floor
New York, NY 10017 3204
☎ 682-7440
Dedicated to AIDS research, policy and education, AMFAR was founded by Elizabeth Taylor.

BODY POSITIVE

2095 Broadway, Suite 306
New York, NY 10023
☎ 566-7333;
Hotline: ☎ (800)566-6599
A community based, volunteer organization created, and run by and for people affected by HIV. Publishes *Body Positive*, a monthly magazine. Holds orientation, gay socials and Tea Dances at The Center for HIV+ gay men and their friends.

BROADWAY CARES/ EQUITY FIGHTS AIDS

165 West 46th Street, Suite 1300
New York, NY 10036
☎ 840-0770; Fax: 840-0551
BC/EFA has led the entertainment industry in the fight against AIDS under the slogan "Imagine, demand and work for a cure." All monies collected go directly or indirectly to providing assistance and services to people with AIDS. Among its many fundraising efforts are three annual events: The Broadway Flea Market; Gypsy of the Year Competition, and the Easter Bonnet Competition. Sporadically BC/EFA holds Broadway Bares, a highly popular event when show boys and girls from current Broadway strip down to their dance belts. A great way to get your thrills while supporting a worthy cause!

COMMUNITY RESEARCH INITIATIVE ON AIDS (CRIA)

275 Seventh Avenue, 20th Floor,
New York, NY 10001
☎ 924-3934; Fax: 924-3936
A non profit AIDS research center dedicated to the study of new treatments for HIV related diseases. Its stated goal is to improve the length and quality of life for people with AIDS/HIV through clinical research.

GAY MEN'S HEALTH CRISIS

129 West 20th Street
New York, NY 10011
☎ 337-3593;
AIDS Hotline: ☎ 807-6655
Website: http://www.gmhc.org
(see also Chapter 9)

GMHC was founded in 1981 by a group of gay men, including Larry Kramer and novelist Edmund White, at a time when no one cared that gay men were beginning to die of a disease that didn't even have a name. Now the largest AIDS organization in the country, GMHC's client base includes women and heterosexuals with AIDS as well as gay men. Less militant than ACT UP, GMHC is unparalleled in the services it provides the community.

Foremost in the field of AIDS education, GMHC conducts workshops and seminars and develops and distributes information on AIDS, risk reduction, safer sex, medical and psychological issues, testing, health insurance and legal issues. They've even published a series of safer sex comics strips. The organization has instituted several Crisis Intervention Programs, including the Buddy Program, comprising volunteers who help PWAs that are unable to handle their daily chores. GMHC provides its clients with group counseling, financial aid, free meals, therapeutic recreational programs and medical referrals. It also lobbies the government for increased AIDS funding and quicker approval of AIDS treatments. Annual fundraisers for the group are the AIDS Walkathon, the Danceathon and the Fire Island Morning Party.

GOD'S LOVE WE DELIVER

895 Amsterdam Avenue
New York, NY 10025
☎ 865-6500

A volunteer organization which delivers hot meals to homebound people with AIDS. In May of 1985 Ganga Stone, then a hospice worker, visited a young man with AIDS at his home. He had no money, had not had a meal for two days, and didn't even have the strength to prepare the groceries that Stone had brought him. That very day she founded God's Love We Deliver.

HOUSING WORKS, INC.

594 Broadway, 7th Floor
New York, NY 10012
☎ 966-0466

Provides housing and support for homeless people living with AIDS and HIV.

METRO NEW YORK QUILTERS

102 Christopher Street, Apt. 4E
New York, NY 10014
☎ 675-7782

A New York group which sews panels of remembrance for the San Francisco-based International AIDS Quilt.

MINORITY TASK FORCE ON AIDS

475 Riverside Drive, Suite 1374
New York, NY 10115
☎ 870-2691; Fax: 870-2607

MOCA: MEN OF COLOR AIDS PREVENTION PROGRAM

125 Worth Street, Box 67
Room 1100, New York, NY 10013
☎ 788-4405; Fax: 788-9661

OUT OF THE CLOSET THRIFT SHOP

220 East 81st Street
New York, NY 10028
☎ 472-3573

A volunteer run organization which sells donated art, antiques, books, clothing, jewelry etc. to fundraise for the gay and lesbian community and AIDS organizations.

PEOPLE WITH AIDS COALITION (PWAC)

50 West 17th Street
New York, NY 10011
☎ 647-1415
PWA staffed hotline: ☎ 647-1420 or (800) 828-3280
Mon-Fri, 10:00am 8:00pm.

A self help organization of people living with AIDS and HIV. Publishes a monthly newsletter.

PEOPLE WITH AIDS HEALTH GROUP

150 West 26th Street, Suite 201
New York, NY 10001
☎ 255-0520; Fax: 255-2080
Email:pwahg@aidsnyc.org
Website: http://www.aidsnyc.org/pwahg

A buyers club for experimental AIDS treatments. Publishes *Notes From the Underground,* six times a year.

POWARS, INC. (PET OWNERS WITH AIDS/ARC RESOURCE SERVICE)

☎ 246-6307

A volunteer group which offers total care service for the pets of people with AIDS.

TREATMENT ACTION GROUP (TAG)

210 East 10th Street, # 601
New York, NY 10003
☎ 260-0300; Fax: 260-8561

Advocacy group devoted to supporting more and better AIDS research.

VISUAL AIDS

131 West 24th Street
New York, NY 10011
☎ 206-6758; Fax: 206-8159

Founded by a group of art professionals to increase awareness about AIDS and promote action to end the Crisis. The Visual Aids Artists' Caucus conceived of the Ribbon Project — a 6" strip of red ribbon folded at the top to make an inverted "V" shape — which is now an international symbol showing commitment to the fight against AIDS. Although wearing a red ribbon has been criticized in some quarters as being nothing more than a politically correct fashion statement, the ribbon has made a significant impact on the general public since its first appearance in 1991.

Among Visual Aids' other projects is Day Without Art, which coincides with World AIDS Day (December 1). Museums, galleries, theaters, and other art venues join together on this day to present lectures and cultural events to focus on the needs of PWAs and the devastation of AIDS. On the evening of Day Without Art, Night Without Light, the entire skyline of Manhattan is dimmed during a symbolic 15 minute blackout to reflect the tragic losses due to AIDS. The project now includes other cities in the US as well.

POLITICS/ LEGAL/ ACTIVIST

ACT UP (AIDS Coalition to Unleash Power)

(see above)

ACLU (American Civil Liberties Union) LESBIAN AND GAY RIGHTS PROJECT

132 West 43rd Street
New York, NY 10036
☎ 944-9800 ext. 545

COALITION FOR LESBIAN AND GAY RIGHTS (CLGR)

The Center
☎ 627-1398

EMPIRE STATE PRIDE AGENDA

611 Broadway, Room 907A
New York, NY 10012
☎ 673-5417

A statewide lesbian and gay political organization which helps to advance legislation important to the community through endorsing candidates for elected office and lobbying the New York state legislature and the city council.

GLAAD (GAY AND LESBIAN ALLIANCE AGAINST DEFAMATION)/NEW YORK

150 West 26th Street
New York, NY 10001
☎ 807-1700

An organization dedicated to combating stereotypes and misinformation about gays and lesbians, GLAAD organizes grass-roots responses to public bigotry and works with the media to improve coverage of gay and lesbian issues. The organization's past efforts include successfully persuading *The New York Times* to change their editorial policy and use the term "gay" for homosexuals, and persuading the Empire State Building management to light up in lavender the city's landmark during Pride Weekend every June.

GAY AND LESBIAN INDEPENDENT DEMOCRATS (GLID)

The Center
☎ 645-1849

LAMBDA LEGAL DEFENSE & EDUCATION FUND

666 Broadway
New York, NY 10012
☎ 995-8585
Founded in 1973, Lambda Legal Defense is the nation's oldest and largest non profit organization working to protect the civil and legal rights of gays, lesbians and people with HIV/AIDS.

LESBIAN AND GAY LAW ASSOCIATION OF GREATER NEW YORK (LeGal)

799 Broadway
New York, NY 10003
☎ 353-9118

LESBIAN & GAY CAUCUS WORKERS WORLD PARTY

55 West 17th Street
New York, NY 10011
☎ 255-0352

LOG CABIN CLUB - NYC

P.O. Box 1690 Madison Square Station, New York, NY 10159
☎ 886-1893
Lesbian and gay Republican club. We are indeed everywhere!

LESBIAN AND GAY IMMIGRATION AND ASYLUM TASK FORCE

☎ 995-8585

STONEWALL DEMOCRATIC CLUB

P.O. Box 1750, Old Chelsea Station, New York, NY 10011
☎ 969-8854

STONEWALL REPUBLICANS

☎ 924-0269

STONEWALL VETERANS ASSOCIATION

☎ 362-6288
A group for the participants of the 1969 Stonewall riots.

PEOPLE OF COLOR/RACIAL & ETHNIC MINORITIES

ASIANS AND FRIENDS — NEW YORK (AFNY)

Box 3361, New York, NY 10163
☎ (718) 488-0630
Promotes friendship among Asian/ Pacific Islander, Asian American and non Asian gay men. Publishes *AFNY News Forum*, a monthly newsletter. They meet every third Saturday at the Center.

BISEXUAL, LESBIAN AND GAY HAITIANS

P.O. Box 1302
New York, NY 10159
☎ (718) 965-3354

THE CAIROS PROJECT
301 Cathedral Parkway
Annex Bldg, Suite 287
New York, NY 10026
☎ 316-2217
Produces *Colorlife*, a monthly magazine with news items, features, interviews and current events calendar "for lesbian, gay, two spirit and bisexual people of color."

CLAN AN UABHAIR
☎ 726-1419
A Gay Scottish society for anyone claiming Scottish ancestry or an interest in Scottish culture.

GAY AND LESBIAN ARABS
☎ 663-9758

GAY & LESBIAN ASSOCIATION OF CUBAN EXILES (GLACE)
P.O. Box 232, New York, NY 10108
☎ Jose at (718) 507-4138

GAY ASIAN AND PACIFIC ISLANDER MEN OF NEW YORK (GAPIMNY)
P.O. Box 830, New York, NY 10002
☎ Scott at 932-8184

GAY MEN OF AFRICAN DESCENT, INC. (GMAD)
133 West 4th Street
New York, NY 10012
☎ 420-0773; Fax: 982-1182

GREEK GAY & LESBIAN ASSOCIATION (GGALA)
☎ 539-6675

IRISH LESBIAN AND GAY ASSOCIATION (IGLO)
P.O. Box 4726, Rockefeller Center Station, NY 10185
☎ 967-7711, Extension 3078

ISRAELIS AND FRIENDS
P.O. Box 1157
Forest Hills, NY 11375
☎ 726-1681

KAMBAL SA LUSOG: PILIPINAS LESBIANS BISEXUALS AND GAYS FOR PROGRESS
P.O. Box 602, FDR Station
New York, NY 10150
☎ Paul at 353-8537

LATINO GAY MEN OF NEW YORK
P.O. Box 1103, Cathedral Station
New York, NY 10025
☎ 663-9148

LAVENDER & GREEN ALLIANCE
☎ (718) 739-2012, Attn: Brendan
A group for Irish and Irish-American gay men and lesbians.

MEN OF ALL COLORS TOGETHER/NEW YORK (MACT)
P.O. Box 1518, Ansonia Station
New York, NY 10023
☎ 330-7678

POLISH LESBIANS AND GAYS TOGETHER
☎ 604-4928

THE SOUTH ASIAN LESBIAN AND GAY ASSOCIATION (SALGA)
P.O Box 50, Cooper Station
New York, NY 10276-0050
☎ 294-2555
Email: salganyc@dorsai.org

VENEZUELAN GAY & LESBIAN ASSOCIATION
☎ 353-1274

WAZOBIA
P.O. Box 255, New York, NY 10116
☎ Nguru: 690-3705
A network of continental African lesbian/gay/bisexual/transgendered people in New York City.

WE WAH & BAR CHEE AMPE: NATIVE TWO SPIRITS (Native American Gays and Lesbians)
☎ 598-0100, ext. 242

RELIGION

AXIOS EASTERN AND ORTHODOX CHRISTIANS
P.O. Box 756, Village Station
New York, NY 10014
☎ Call Nick at(718) 805-1952
A social and support group for gay and lesbian Armenian, Greek and Russian Orthodox Christians as well as for Eastern Rite Catholics, which meets at The Center on the 2nd Friday of every month at 8:00pm.

BUDDHIST LESBIANS & GAYS: MAITRI DORJE
☎ 619-4099

CHRISTIAN SCIENCE GROUP
☎ 532-8379
Gay and lesbian study group which meets at The Center on Thursdays 8:00pm-9:00pm.

CONGREGATION BETH SIMCHAT TORAH (Lesbian and Gay Synagogue)
57 Bethune Street
New York, NY 10024
(West & Washington Streets)
☎ 929-9498
Situated in the Westbeth Housing Complex in the West Village. Provides High Holy Day and Friday evening services, Jewish/AIDS

outreach and educational, cultural, social, spiritual and feminist programming.

CONGREGATION B'NAI JESHURUN

270 West 89th Street
New York, NY 10023
☎ 787-7600

Conservative synagogue. Services are currently held at the Church of St. Paul and St. Andrew at West 86th Street (at West End Avenue), Friday evening services are especially popular. B'nai Jeshurun has a large gay and lesbian membership.

DIGNITY

There are two active Manhattan chapters of the fellowship of lesbian, gay, bisexual and transgender Roman Catholics:

DIGNITY/BIG APPLE

P.O. Box 1028, Old Chelsea Station, New York, NY 10011
☎ 818-1309

Liturgy and social gathering at The Center on Saturdays and 8:00pm.

DIGNITY/NEW YORK

P.O. Box 1554, FDR Station
New York, NY 10150
☎ 627-6488

Worship services and social on Sunday evenings, 7:30pm at St.John's in the Village Episcopal Church, 218 West 11th Street (at Waverly Place).

INTEGRITY/NEW YORK GAY & LESBIAN EPISCOPALIANS

Box 5202, New York, NY 10185
☎ (718) 720-3054

Founded in 1975, the group meets on Thursdays at 7:30pm at the Church of St. Luke in the Fields (487 Hudson Street, ☎ 924 0562). Integrity established the National AIDS Memorial at the Cathedral of St. John the Divine and raises funds for AIDS charities.

MARANATHA

at Riverside Church
490 Riverside Drive at 120th Street
☎ 222-5900

Gay, lesbian and bisexual group affiliated with Riverside Church Arranges a worship service on Gay Pride Sunday followed by an annual Pride Breakfast.

METROPOLITAN COMMUNITY CHURCH OF NEW YORK (MCC)

446 West 36th Street/8th & 9th Avenues, New York, NY 10018
☎ 629-7440

A non denominational gay and lesbian Christian group which holds Sunday Services at 10:00am and 7:00pm.

RADICAL FAERIES
P.O. Box 1251
New York, NY 10013
☎ (718) 625-4505
A community dedicated to non western traditions of spiritual growth, respect for nature, magic, pagan ritual, drag and celebration of life.

STEPHEN WISE FREE SYNAGOGUE
30 West 68th Street
New York, NY 10023
☎ 877-4050
An open Reform synagogue which encourages lesbians and gays to actively participate in their worship services and social functions.

UNITY FELLOWSHIP CHURCH
P.O. Box 2708
New York, NY 10008
☎ (718) 636-5646
Non denominational church primarily for Black lesbians and gays, although open to everybody.

SUPPORT

BISEXUAL GAY & LESBIAN YOUTH OF NY (BiGLYNY)
☎ 620-7310

BISEXUAL MEN OF ALL CULTURES (BiMAC)
☎ 459-4784

GAY FATHERS FORUM
P.O. Box 1321, Midtown Station
New York, NY 10018
☎ 721-4216

GIRLS NIGHT OUT
Box 369, Brooklyn, NY 11235
☎ (201) 794-1665, ext. 201
A group for transgender, transvestites and transsexuals.

IMPERIAL COURT OF NEW YORK
☎ 475-0838
Part of an international network, the Court sponsors Night of 1,000 Gowns — an annual fundraising drag ball, which is held on the last Saturday in March.

IMPERIAL QUEENS & KINGS OF NEW YORK
☎ 229-1968 (days); 627-1869 (evenings)
A support organization for drag queens and transsexuals.

NORTH AMERICAN MAN/ BOY LOVE ASSOCIATION (NAMBLA)
P.O. Box 174, Midtown Station
New York, NY 10018
☎ 807-8578
The controversial and legally challenged intergenerational group, produces monthly newsletter.

PARENTS & FRIENDS OF LESBIANS & GAYS (P FLAG)
P.O. Box 553, Lennox Hill Station
New York, NY 10021
☎ 463-0629

PRIME TIMERS
P.O. Box 291, Midtown Station
New York, NY 10011
☎ 929-1035
A club for gay men over 50 and their friends which holds biweekly meetings, social outings, erotic parties, and produces a monthly newsletter.

SAGE (Senior Action in a Gay Environment)
305 7th Avenue
New York, NY 10001
☎ 741-2247; Fax: 366-1947
An organization dedicated to the care and support of senior members of the lesbian and gay community. Men's 50+ rap group Wednesday 5:30pm, Friday 6:00pm; Men's 40+ rap group Thursday 7:00pm.

DISABLED

EDGE: EDUCATION IN A DISABLED GAY ENVIRONMENT
P.O. Box 305, Village Station
New York, NY 10014
☎ 929-7178; Attn: Carl Eden

EMPIRE RAINBOW ALLIANCE OF THE DEAF
c/o Fennell
117 Christopher Street, Apt 12
New York, NY 10014

PROFESSIONALS

FIRE FLAG
☎ (914) 762-6261
An organization for gay and lesbian fire fighters, meets at The Center.

GAY & LESBIAN PSYCHIATRISTS OF NEW YORK (GLPNY)
Box 1389, Old Chelsea Station
New York, NY 10113
☎ 265-5539

GAY & LESBIAN SOCIAL WORKERS
☎ 989-6083

GAY OFFICERS ACTION LEAGUE (GOAL)
☎ 996-8808
The most poular members of New York City's Police force.

GAY PILOTS ASSOCIATION
☎ (718) 459-6168

LESBIAN AND GAY TEACHERS ASSOCIATION OF NEW YORK CITY
☎ (718) 596-1864
Email: LGTA@aol.com

NATIONAL LESBIAN & GAY JOURNALISTS ASSOCIATION/NEW YORK (NLGJA)
☎ 629-2045
Email: NLGJANY@aol.com

NEW YORK ADVERTISING & COMMUNICATIONS NETWORK, INC. (NYACN)
Box 149, 494A Hudson Street
New York, NY 10014
☎ 517-0380

NEW YORK BANKERS GROUP
☎ 807-9584, ext. 24

ORGANIZATION OF LESBIAN & GAY ARCHITECTS & DESIGNERS (OLGAD)
Box 927, Old Chelsea Station New York, NY 10113
☎ 475-7652

OUT IN FILM
501 Madison Avenue, 19th Floor
New York, NY 10022
☎ 877-6443
Organization of Lesbian and Gay Filmmakers.

RECOVERY/THERAPY

ALCOHOLICS ANONYMOUS
☎ 647-1680
Some meetings held at The Center, call for schedule.

COCAINE ANONYMOUS
☎ 496-4266

IDENTITY HOUSE
39 West 14th Street
Mailing address: P.O.Box 572
Old Chelsea Station
New York, NY 10011
☎ 243-8181
Peer counseling and therapy referral center for the lesbian, gay and bisexual community.

OVEREATERS ANONYMOUS LESBIAN & GAY GROUP
Box 2121, Grand Central Station
New York, NY 10163
☎ 348-7474

SEXUAL COMPULSIVES ANONYMOUS (SCA)
P.O. Box 1585, Old Chelsea Station, New York, NY 10011
☎ 439-1123

LEATHER/ LEVI & S/M

BLACK LEATHER
☎ 222-9794; Fax: 777-5349, Attn: Lidell Jackson

BROTHERS IN LEATHER
☎ 714-0596; Fax 564-6117, Attn: Darrell
For men of color who are into leather/fetish lifestyle.

GAY MALE S/M ACTIVISTS (GMSMA)

496A Hudson Street, Suite D23
New York, NY 10014
☎ 727-9878

Founded in 1981, GMSMA is dedicated to safe and responsible S/M and holds open meetings with programs on S/M techniques, lifestyle issues and political concerns. Meets on the 2nd and 4th Wednesdays of every month, September through June at The Center.

NATIONAL LEATHER ASSOCIATION — METRO NEW YORK CHAPTER

P.O. Box 1084
New York, NY 10156
☎ (718) 597-0019

Pan-sexual group, with some events at Cell Block 28 (see Chapter 8).

OTHERS

GAY, LESBIAN & BISEXUAL VETERANS OF GREATER NEW YORK (GLBVETS)

346 Broadway, Suite 811
New York, NY 10013
☎ 349-3455

GIRTH AND MIRTH CLUB OF NEW YORK

P.O. Box 10, Dept. G
Pelham, NY 10803
☎ (914) 699-7735

"For heavy chubby men and the men who like them." Publishes the *Fat Apple Review*, a monthly newsletter. Meets every Thursday at Mike's Bar and has a monthly socials at The Center.

M.A.N. MALES AU NATUREL

332 Bleecker Street
P.O. Box 133, New York, NY 10014
☎ 535-3914

Members only, gay male "non sexual" nudist group established to provide an atmosphere for "social fraternization unencumbered by clothing in a variety of indoor and outdoor settings appropriate to the season."

TIMES SQUARES, NYC SQUARE DANCE CLUB

P.O. Box 1229, Ansonia Station
New York, NY 10023
☎ 873-3962

Meets every Tuesday night at PS 3 at Hudson and Christopher Streets, 7:30pm-10:30pm, and at the Fashion Institute of Technology (Seventh Avenue at 27th Street) June September. Call for more locations.

copyright © Michael Huhn, taken from the book:
MICHAEL HUHN PHOTOS, Éditions Aubrey Walter

8: MEETING MEN

The city of such young men, I swear I cannot live happy without I often go talk, walk, eat, drink, sleep with them!

— Walt Whitman, "Mannahatta"
[*Leaves of Grass*, 1860 version]

Whatever you're looking for, you can be sure you'll find it here in this city. From romance to raunch, it's all part of the New York scene.

You'll have no trouble meeting the local boys. Most New Yorkers are naturally curious and love to meet out-of-towners. They delight in hearing new accents, and I even know a few who like to collect foreigners like postage stamps! And, of course, there are the practical-minded men who know that friends in other countries can come in very handy when travelling abroad.

BARS

Most of New York's gay bars are concentrated in the West Village, the East Village and Chelsea. Others are scattered through the midtown area; there are a couple on the Upper West Side. Most bars open at four in the afternoon (noon on Sundays) and close at 4:00am. When you go bar hopping bear in mind that most bars fill up around happy hour (usually between 4:00pm and 8:00pm on weekdays when drinks are two for the price of one) and then again around 11:30pm. You are likely to encounter the largest crowds on weekends, but some bars attract hordes of thirsty boys on weeknights by offering drink specials (Remember it's customary to leave a tip of at least $1 for the bar tender — more if he's cute and he flirts with you!).

The legal drinking age in New York State is twenty-one. Getting *carded* or *proofed* means being asked to show proper identification to prove you are of age. Don't take drinks out onto the street — it's against the law.

The city's several women's bars and clubs are not included in the listings below. For up-to-date information refer to *HX*, *Next* or *The Native*. All telephone numbers in these listings are in the 212 area code unless otherwise specified.

DOWNTOWN: East Village

THE BAR

68 2nd Avenue/ 4th Street
☎ 674-9714
Your typical East Village bar with plain black walls, a juke box and pool table. Don't let the "no-frills" aesthetic fool you, this popular bar attracts a diverse, young crowd.

BOILER ROOM

86 East 4th Street/ 2nd Avenue
☎ 254-7536
Just around the corner from The Bar, a new addition to the East Village scene, with pool table and juke-box. It's jam-packed on the weekends with students and an attractive young crowd.

CAKE

99 Avenue B/ 7th Street
☎ 674-7957
Cover charge on some nights
Concrete and exposed brick, plush sofas, and a dark basement— a brand new venue that's become very popular with both the horny boys and drag queens of the East Village.

CROWBAR

339 East 10th Street/
Avenues A&B
☎ 420-0670
There are parties every night (varying cover charge) at this very popular, newly refurbished East Village hole-in-the-wall. Catch *The Hedda Lettuce Show*, a popular cable television drag chat show which is taped live at Crowbar on Monday nights.

DICK'S BAR

192 Second Avenue/ 12th Street
☎ 475-2071
Dick's Bar has a pool table, juke box and pinball machine, but although it is larger than the other bars in the area, it's not as popular.

TUNNEL BAR

116 1st Avenue/ 7th Street

☎ 777-9232

Small but lively neighborhood bar with a pool table as well. Different theme nights during the week. Porno video nights facilitate good cruising. Monday night is for show tune queens.

WONDER BAR

505 East 6th Street/ Avenue A

☎ 777-9105

A small, casual hangout with a large screen video projection which attracts a convivial, mixed crowd. On the weekends, when some of the other East Village venues get too crowded, you can sit down for a quiet drink with a new friend at Wonder Bar.

DOWNTOWN: West Village

BAR d'O

29 Bedford Street

☎ 627-1580

There is generally a mixed crowd at this funky cabaret lounge and bar. But on the nights drag diva Joey Arias, best known for "channelling" Billie Holliday, holds court, the clientele is mostly gay.

BOOTS & SADDLE

76 Christopher Street

☎ 929-9684

A Western style, neighborhood watering hole whose heyday was in the 70s. Older crowd.

DUGOUT

185 Christopher Street

☎ 242-9113

A place for serious pool players and older neighborhood clientele. A predominantly leather crowd gathers here on Sunday afternoons.

HANGAR BAR

115 Christopher Street

☎ 627-2044

This old venue with a face lift and a new name on "gay main street" has become very popular (especially on the hot n' horny "ManFridays"). The airplane hangar design with high ceilings provides a welcome feeling of large open spaces.

JULIUS'

159 West 10th Street/ Waverly Place

☎ 929-9672

Julius' Tavern, the oldest bar in the village, attracts a mature crowd. Before it became a gay bar, Julius' was targeted in 1966 by three members of the Mattachine Society, the first gay organization in the U.S., who organized a "sip-in" to challenge the law that forbade bartenders from serving professed homosexuals. Hustlers from the now defunct Ninth Circle operate from here.

KELLER'S

384 West Street/ Barrow Street

☎ 243-1907

A predominantly African-American bar near the Hudson River front. Popular among the mostly Black and Latino crowd which hangs out at the nearby Christopher Street pier on weekends.

THE LURE

409 West 13th Street/ 9th Avenue

☎ 741-3919

Website: http://www.thelure.com

New York's newest and most popular fetish bar; the name spells Leather Uniforms Rubber Etc. A strict leather/levi/rubber/uniform code enforced on Fridays and Saturdays. On Wednesday nights Lure hosts Pork, a slutty party for leathermen of all ages, featuring live S&M/fetish performances.

MARIE'S CRISIS

59 Grove Street/ Seventh Avenue South

☎ 243-9323

You can sing-along with a mixed crowd show tunes from *The Boyfriend* to *The Phantom of the Opera* at this cramped but cozy, low-ceilinged piano bar.

MIKE'S CLUB CAFE

400 West 14th Street/ 9th Avenue

☎ 691-6606

Located near the 14th Street sex clubs, where the meat-packing district ends and Chelsea begins. Mike's large french doors which open out into the street create a pleasantly airy and comfortable ambiance.

THE MONSTER

80 Grove Street/ Sheridan Square

☎ 924-3558

A Greenwich Village institution, this neighborhood bar with a piano on the street level and a disco in the basement gets very crowded on weeknights. The Monster is the only place to dance in the Christopher Street neighborhood and is open every night (cover charge varies). Sunday is Latin night.

NUTS & BOLTS LOUNGE

101 7th Avenue

☎ 620-4000

Laid-back lounge bar with comfortable seating; outrageously campy Karaoke nights on Wednesdays and Fridays.

PIECES

8 Christopher Street

☎ 929-9291

A neighborhood bar with pool table and videos. The clientele is younger and more diverse than those of the bars further west on Christopher Street.

SNEAKERS

392 West Street/ Christopher & West 10th Streets

☎ 242-9830

This venerable dive, around the corner from the western end of the Christopher Street strip, attracts a largely Black crowd.

STONEWALL

53 Christopher Street

☎ 463-0950

The site of the historic Stonewall Inn where the momentous events of 1969 took place. Various establishments such as a bagel shop and a clothing boutique occupied this spot until it reopened as a gay bar in 1991. Crowd is an eclectic mix with pool playing regulars.

TWO POTATO

145 Christopher Street/ Greenwich Street

☎ 255-0286

The most popular Black and Hispanic bar in the city. A cover of $4 (which includes one drink) is charged from 8:00pm.

TY'S

114 Christopher Street/ Bedford Street

☎ 741-9641

A neighborhood watering hole for a mature crowd. You may think you have walked through a time warp into the 70s.

UNCLE CHARLIE'S

56 Greenwich Avenue

☎ 255-8787

Once Charlie's was every new boy in town's first gay bar. Now that the Chelsea bars set gay fashion, Charlie's is no longer trendy. But the crowd is an interesting mix, ethnically and generationally. The videos, go-go boys, "hard-body" contests and Thursday Latino nights are popular. The toilets here are spacious and clean if you need to go when you are in the Village.

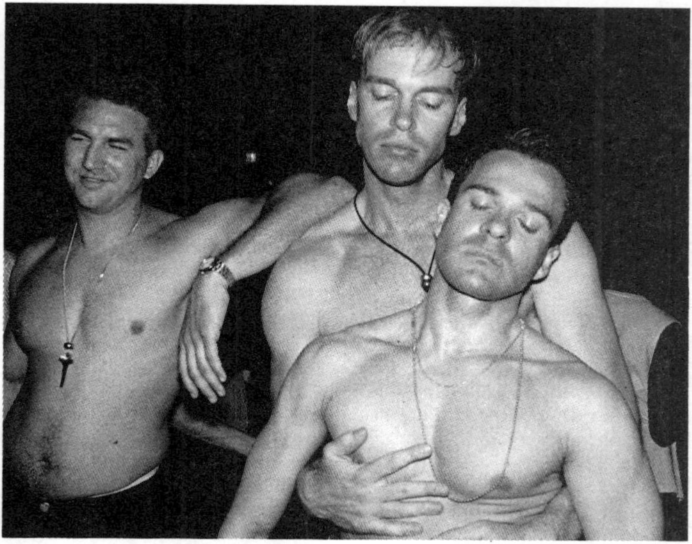

photo copyright © Tina Paul

DOWNTOWN: Chelsea

BARRACUDA

275 West 22nd Street/ 8th Avenue
☎ 645-8613

A new and highly popular addition to the Chelsea gay scene. Attracts a friendly mix of drag queens and muscle boys — Chelsea meets the East Village. Cruise in the front bar and lounge in the comfy couches at the back. Despite the smoke and loud music, the lounge section could be the perfect place to start getting intimate with a new friend.

THE BREAK

232 8th Avenue/ 22nd Street
☎ 627-0072

Small and cruisy, this neighborhood stand-up bar attracts the full spectrum of Chelsea's younger gay men. On Thursdays, when margaritas cost a dollar, there's a line to get in.

CHAMPS
17 West 19th Street/ 5th Avenue
☎ 633-1717
Designed to remind you of your high school gym fantasies, Champs attracts an appropriately pumped-up crowd. You can grope a friendly jock on the raunchy "Locker Room" Wednesday nights.

THE EAGLE
142 Eleventh Avenue/ 21st Street
☎ 691-8451
One of the city's stalwart leather/ levi cruise bars. No strict dress code is enforced but if you dress too preppy you will stick out like a sore thumb; no drag allowed. Pool table for serious players.

KING
579 Sixth Avenue/ 16th Street
☎ 366-5464
A new three-level playground that quickly established itself on the Chelsea scene. There's a bar on the first floor with dancing on the second. If you are in a sleazy mood, King's third floor "private attic" (open on some nights with varying cover charges), the shameless lap-dancers and go-go boys, and the Wednesday night amateur strip contests will not disappoint you.

RAWHIDE
212 Eighth Avenue/ 21st Street
☎ 242-9332
Western-style levi/leather bar which opens at 8:00am. For some the first stop on the way west to the Spike or Eagle. Pool table.

ROME
290 8th Avenue/ 24th Street
☎ 242-6969
The theme of this recently opened two-level watering hole on the northern edge of Chelsea is Imperial Rome: The hunky waiters are dressed like Roman soldiers in short leather skirts; mirrors, marble and frescoes provide a suitably decadent touch.

SPIKE
120 Eleventh Avenue/ 20th Street
☎ 243-9688
The flagship of the New York leather scene, although it has been somewhat eclipsed by The Lure. Dress code is leather, western or uniform, but T-shirts and jeans are tolerated. Note how the leathermen stay on the left side of the bar and the clean-cut hunks congregate near the pool table. Do the twain ever meet? On weekend nights, the spillover from the Spike will often flow into the Eagle across the street, creating the twin bar scene the regulars call "The Speagle".

SPLASH
50 West 17th Street/ 6th Avenue
☎ 691-0073
This large swanky bar has been renovated to provide extra cruising space. Part of the entertainment at Splash features go-go boys who take real showers in elevated glass booths. Check out the urinals downstairs which are individually equipped with mini television

screens. Perhaps less trendy than it was a few years ago among the city's good-looking "guppies" (gay urban professionals) and muscle queens, Splash still packs a attractive crowd on weekends. "Musical Mondays" are reserved for showtunes.

TREE HOUSE CLUB

254 West 23rd Street/ 8th Avenue

Scheduled to open in June 1996. Tree House promises to be Chelsea's first piano bar and restaurant (with outdoor garden).

MIDTOWN: East Side

REGENTS

317 East 53rd Street/ 2nd Avenue

☎ 593-3091

A brand new "gentleman's club" and restaurant, this upscale sister to The Townhouse insists on "proper attire" for its clientele. Time will tell if Regents will become an elegant replacement for Rounds, the now defunct hustler bar which used to be located next door.

SOUTH DAKOTA

405 Third Avenue/ 29th Street

☎ 684-8376

Strictly neighborhood bar with pool table and pinball machine. You'll find a widely diverse crowd and a congenial atmosphere.

THE TOWNHOUSE

236 East 58th/ 3rd Avenue

☎ 754-4649

With its wallpaper, stuffed chairs, carpeting, oak bar and live piano music, the Townhouse is unique in the New York bar scene. The age of the crowd can be very mixed tending towards older gentlemen. But you will also find young professionals in suits and other young men who may or may not be (very discreetly) for hire.

THE WEB

40 East 58th Street/ Park & Madison Avenues

☎ 308-1546

Formerly Club 58, a place for Asian men to meet other Asians, and also the Caucasians who admire them. Predominantly young crowd. Go-go dancers and drag shows on weekends. Dancing on the lower level, cover charge on some nights. (See also CLUBS)

MIDTOWN: West Side

BUSTERS

818 10th Avenue/ 54th Street

☎ 245-2790

Neighborhood hangout in Hell's Kitchen. Popular with cross-dressers on the weekend.

CATS BAR

232 West 48th Street/ 8th Avenue

☎ 245-5245

A small and tacky bar which attracts midtown trade. Strip shows on weekends.

CLEO'S NINTH AVENUE SALOON

656 9th Avenue/ 46th Street
☎ 307-1503
A neighborhood bar located near the theater district. Congenial and low-key, it's a good place to take a date for an after-theater drink before going to your place or his.

SALLY'S

252 West 43rd Street/ 8th Avenue
☎ 391-0713
New York's premier transvestite and transsexual bar, located next door to the entrance of the Hotel Carter and across the street from the offices of *The New York Times*. Get the bartender's advice if you want to spend time with one of the "working girls." There are shows every night for which a cover of $10 (includes one drink) is charged after 8:30pm.

THE SAVOY

335 West 41st Street/ 9th Avenue
☎ 560-9635
Mostly Latin and Black crowd. Situated next door to the Port Authority bus terminal, The Savoy gets its share of Times Square tourists and the local hustlers who make money off them.

STELLA'S

266 West 47th Street/ 8th Avenue
☎ 575-1680
Recently opened and retaining some of the style of the restaurant which previously occupied the space, Stella's is poised to become an upscale venue for the midtown trade. Remember many of the attractive boys hanging about may be working. There is a cover charge on certain nights.

UPTOWN: West Side

CANDLE BAR

309 Amsterdam Avenue/ 74th Street
☎ 874-9155
Western-style bar populated with a mostly mature crowd, neighborhood regulars and serious pool players.

THE WORKS

428 Columbus Avenue/ 81st Street
☎ 799-7365
The Works is the uptown counterpart of Chelsea's The Break. From guppies to Columbia students, this stand-up bar is the place to meet the young gay men of the Upper West Side. Very cruisy in the late evenings, the crowds are largest on Thursdays and the weekends. As the evening wears on, some who haven't made connections at the bar make a short trip up the block to Les Hommes Bookshop (see VIDEO BOOTH STORES below), to socialize on a slightly different level.

CLUBS, DISCOS, DANCES

It's hard to keep track of the clubs in New York — today's hot spot could be passé tomorrow and maybe closed a month or two later. Often a new club springs up in the old venue under a different name and the cycle starts all over again. To stay abreast of the ever changing scene refer to the gay publications listed in Chapter 7. Club hours are usually from 11:00pm to 4:00am, with the crowds arriving around midnight. After-hours clubs, which serve no alcohol, hit their peak at about 5:00am. The admission rates listed below are full price, but keep an eye out for flyers or invitations that will get you in free or for a reduced rate into some clubs at off-peak hours.

WHERE THE BOYS GO, NEW YORK CITY, circa May 1996

Monday:	• The Web • King • Champs (Milk) • Irving Plaza (Sugar Babies)
Tuesday:	• Roxy • Crowbar • Jackie 60
Wednesday:	• Limelight • Crowbar • Flamingo East • Champs • The Lure (Pork)
Thursday:	• SFB (Factoria 21) • Cake
Friday:	• Limelight • Crowbar • The Monster • The Web • SFB • Don Hill's (Squeeze Box) • King • Pyramid
Saturday:	• Roxy • The Tunnel • Twilo • SFB • Gotham Rodeo • Monster • The Web
Sunday:	• Palladium (Bump!) • Crowbar • The Monster

Marc Berkley presents
New York at Night
FRIDAYS
Lick It!
at Limelight
2 Dance Floors
2 Lounges
Go Go Dancers
SATURDAYS
Tunnel Featuring
Junior Vasquez
Dancing 'til Noon
The Kenny Scharf Lounge
Drag Queens Galore
Hot Male Dancers
SUNDAYS
Bump!
at Palladium
The Biggest Sunday
in New York
with 100 ft Ceilings
Featuring
New York's Best DJs
Merritt,
Austin,
Carlos Pertuz
& Mark Tarbox
LIMELIGHT
47 West 20th Street
212.807.7850
Tunnel
220 12th Avenue
212.695.4682
MARC BERKLEY'S
Bump!
126 East 14th Street
212.473.7171

CROWBAR

(see also under BARS)
339 East 10th Street/
Avenue A & B
☎ 420-0670
Varying cover charges.
A popular East Village hotspot with dance parties on a different theme each night.

DON HILL'S (SQUEEZE BOX)

511 Greenwich Street
☎ 334-1390
Fridays from 10:00pm, $10
A funky crowd of drag queens, queer boys and girls and curious straights flock every Friday night to this punk and metal party hosted by Mistress Formika.

EDELWEISS

580 Eleventh Avenue/ 43rd Street
☎ 629-1021
Daily from 8:30 pm; $15 after 9:00pm
Male, female, transvestite or transsexual, gay, lesbian or bi, all are welcomed here, though you may not fancy a stroll in this part of the Hell's Kitchen neighborhood after hours.

FLAMINGO EAST (SALON WEDNESDAY)

219 Second Avenue/ 13th Street
☎ 533-2860
Wednesdays from 10:00pm, $3
End of the month dance party, $5
More for hanging out than for dancing, the Salon is one of the coolest and trendiest spots in the East Village.

GOTHAM RODEO

39 West 19th Street, 5th Floor
☎ 243-7837
Saturdays from 9:00pm, $8
Who'd have thought there were so many two-stepping gay cowboys in Manhattan! You can take lessons before the party begins from 8:00-9:00pm.

IRVING PLAZA (SUGAR BABIES)

17 Irving Plaza/ 15th Street
☎ 777-6817
On Mondays from 11:30pm, $6
This mixed, but mostly gay Monday night party for serious dancers has become a popular fixture on the gay weekly calendar.

JACKIE 60 at The Bar Room

432 West 14th/ Washington Street
one block from the Hudson River
☎ 677-6060
Tuesdays from 10:30pm, $10
An eclectic dance club which regularly presents performance art and off-beat readings that attract New York celebs, European club kids and lots of gay boys.

LIMELIGHT

Side Entrance, West 20th Street/
5th & 6th Avenues
☎ 807-7850
Gay nights are Wednesday &
Friday from 11:00pm, $15

Make sure you enter on 20th Street. If you go by the main entrance you'll have to battle your way through hordes of straight teenagers from the suburbs. Housed in the former Church of the Holy Communion, which was built in the 1840s, the controversial nightclub was New York's most trendy spot when it opened in 1984. Limelight's two gay nights are still very popular and the tiny backroom sees a lot of action.

MONSTER

(See also under bars)
80 Grove Street at Sheridan Square
☎ 924-3558
Varying cover charge.

There is dancing every night from 10:00pm in the basement of this West Village neighborhood piano bar and dance club.

PALLADIUM (BUMP!)

126 East 14th Street/ 3rd Avenue
☎ 473-7171
Sundays from 11:00pm, $15

Now located in one of New York's oldest dance clubs, Bump! attracts Manhattan's trendy gay set — flexing gym boys (with their shirts off)as well as club kids dressed in glitter. It's the best Sunday night party in town.

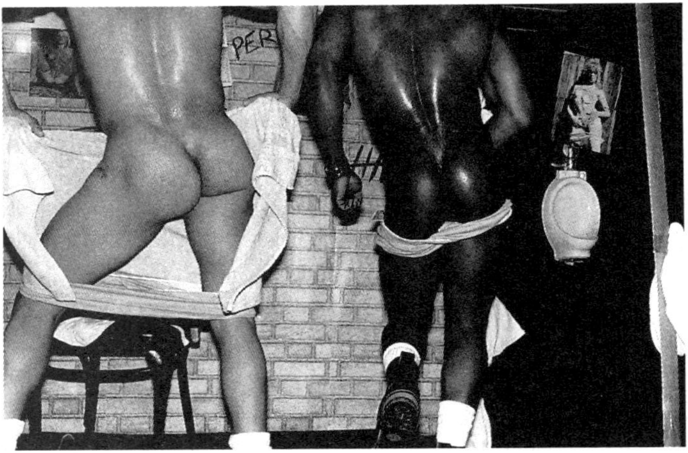

JACKIE 60 photo copyright © Tina Paul

PYRAMID

101 Avenue A/ 6th Street
☎ 473-7184
Saturday: ORIGINAL SIN, from 10:30pm, $10
The Pyramid, which spawned the East Village aesthetic and Wigstock, the annual dragfest, is still a hot venue for trannies, funky boys and adventurous girls.

ROXY

515 West 18th Street/ 10th & 11th Avenues
☎ 645-5156
Tuesdays: POWERSKATE, a roller derby, from 10:00pm, $10
Saturdays: Dancing from 11:00pm, $20
Recently redecorated the Roxy is located at the western edge of Chelsea amidst auto repair shops and warehouses. On Tuesday nights, athletic gay men work up a sweat whizzing by on rollerskates while cruising each other. On Saturday nights, New York's hottest men from muscle queens to drag queens party all night.

SFB

12 West 21st Street/ 5th & 6th Avenues
☎ 206-7770
Thursdays FACTORIA 21, from 11:00pm, $10
Fridays, from 11:00 pm $12
The hypnotic house music at SFB (formerly the Sound Factory Bar) keeps the predominantly Black and Latin crowd dancing till dawn.

THE TUNNEL

midblock at 27th Street between 11th & 12th Avenues
(use the Boy's Entrance)
☎ 695-4682
Saturdays from 11:30pm, $20
The imaginative space can hold 4,000 people. Doors close at 9am but the dancing goes on till noon. The city's premier DJ, Junior Vasquez reigns.

TWILO

530 West 27th Street/ 10th & 11th Avenues
☎ 268-1600
Sat from 11:00pm, $20
Formerly the Sound Factory, Twilo, along with the Roxy and the Tunnel is part of the triumvirate of dance clubs which dominate the Saturday night scene.

THE WEB

(see also under BARS)
40 East 58th Street/ Park & Madison Avenues
☎ 308-1546
Varying cover charges.
Asian boys meet other Asians as well as the white boys who find them interesting. Drag queens and go-go boys provide the floor show entertainment.

top: MISTRESS FORMIKA AT SQUEEZEBOX; bottom: JACKIE 60

OCCASIONAL DANCES

THE CENTER

The Lesbian and Gay Community Center, 208 West 13th Street/ 7th & 8th Avenues
☎ 620-7310
From Sept through June, usually on the 1st and 3rd Sat
9:00pm-1:00am, $8
A very different experience from the frenetic club scene, the Center Dances is ideal for casual socializing and dancing, and is a good introduction for someone new to the scene.

COLUMBIA DANCES

Earl Hall, Columbia University (enter through 116th Street and Broadway and turn left)
First Friday of every month
10:00pm-2:00am, $8
sponsored by the Columbia Lesbian, Bisexual and Gay Coalition,
☎ 854-1488
Hot Columbia students and the ambiance of a college fraternity party make these dances very popular.

THE SAINT-AT-LARGE

The giant disco of the 80s is gone but its spirit lives on in the four Saint-at-Large parties held during the year: THE WHITE PARTY held on the President's Day weekend in February; THE BLACK PARTY held in the last weekend of March; THE HALLOWEEN PARTY in October and THE NEW YEAR'S PARTY. The venues vary, but the parties are always the wildest and hottest in the city. But if you aren't on some sort of high, you just may not get it. Some boys have been known to go on for 24-hours non-stop; the Black Party usually flows into a follow-up party somewhere else the next day. Tickets around $40, ☎ 674-8541 for information.

THE LEATHER AND S/M SCENE

Oldtimers may complain that the city's leather scene isn't what it was in the 70s and early 80s, but there is a new generation that is donning skins, getting into harness and wielding whips in a manner appropriate to the safer but no less horny 90s.

The Lure (with a strict dress code enforced on Fridays and Saturdays) is the 90s equivalent of the notorious Mineshaft and the Anvil which flourished in the heyday of the leather scene. You will also find the leather and levis crowd at **The Spike, The Eagle** and **Rawhide** in Chelsea or some of the older West Village Christopher Street bars, **Hangar Bar** and particularly **The Dugout** on Sunday afternoons. (See BARS above.) **Cell Block 28, The Manhole** and **J's/The Hangout** (see PRIVATE CLUBS below) also cater to the city's leathermen and a S/M clientele.

10th ANNUAL MR. LEATHER CONTEST AT THE ROXY

photo copyright © Tina Paul

The city's premier leather events are **Leather Pride** and the **New York Leather Weekend**. Leather Pride is usually held in June on the weekend prior to Gay Pride, and its highlights are an auction for leather merchandise and The Mr. Drummer Contest. New York Leather Weekend is held in April and culminates with the selection of Mr. Leather New York. (☎ 228-2706 or write c/o John Lunning, 344 East 9th Street, New York, NY 10003 for information.) The Saint-at-Large **Black Party** also draws a large number of leathermen.

If you are new to the leather scene and wish to learn the ropes contact Gay Male S/M Activists (GMSMA), listed in Chapter 7. They conduct workshops for the leather or S/M novice, including classes for tops and bottoms!

See also fetish club listings at the end of this chapter and information on leather shops under EROTICA in Chapter 11.

CRUISING

• If you aren't sure about how to protect yourself against AIDS, please read Chapter 9 on Health before you go out to play. (If you are not from the U.S., you may find the Safer Sex guidelines differ slightly from practices in your own country.)

• Public sex is, of course, against the law and entirely at your own risk. Since the current Republican mayor took office, the police have been cracking down on "public indecency" with greater enthusiasm. The information that follows does not represent endorsement of the practices involved, nor the businesses concerned.

The gayest areas in New York are the West Village (particularly Christopher Street and 7th Avenue between Greenwich Avenue and Bleecker Street); Chelsea (between 14th and 21st Streets on

7th and 8th Avenues) and the Upper West Side (in the area between 65th and 79th Streets on Broadway and Columbus Avenue).

The city parks, like those in most cities in the world, offer the best cruise spots in New York. Manhattan's prime playground for gay men is an area known as the Ramble in Central Park. Originally conceived as a preserve for native plants, the Ramble is a wild, wooded and rocky 37-acre area with twisted paths, nooks and crannies. It is also one of the few heavily wooded spots in Manhattan, and thus attracts many species of birds, and bird watchers, with whom gay men share the Park.

How to get there: From the West Side, enter the Park at West 72nd Street, walk north-east and cross the Park's main drive (the West Drive). When you get to the bridge, the path on the left leads to the Ramble. From 5th Avenue, enter the Park at 72nd Street and walk north-west till you come to the Loeb Boathouse. Follow the uphill path which is flanked by the bicycle rental location. Turn left and you are on the eastern edge of the Ramble.

Activity in the Park is at its peak just before dusk in late spring through early autumn (until the trees shed their leaves). DON'T LINGER IN THE PARK AFTER SUNDOWN. Needless to say, any Park activity in secluded spots is at your own risk, but you are generally safe during the day. Nevertheless, keep your wits about you and do not go into areas which are too isolated, especially if you feel the slightest bit uncomfortable about your partner. Stay close to the perimeters where there are always other people in the park. Leave your wallet at home. (The general street-wise rules in Chapter 2 apply here as well.)

Finally, al fresco sex can be very exciting, but please remember that other people use the Park as well. Be conscious of parents and kids who wander unsuspectingly down the Ramble's paths and also the serious ornithologist intent on tracking a completely different species.

SEX ESTABLISHMENTS

New York City's Department of Health shut down most of the city's gay bathhouses in 1984-85 in the wake of the AIDS Crisis. The early 90s resurgence of sex clubs and backrooms (gay, lesbian and straight) in New York has been curbed recently by conservative city policies and censure from certain parts of the gay community itself. New York State Public Health Law defines both fellatio and anal intercourse as high risk sexual activity. Many sex establishments employ monitors to implement a "lips above the hips" policy. But ultimately no amount of legislating or monitoring is as effective as an individual making his own educated decisions about sex. Have fun, but be safe!

BATHHOUSES

EAST SIDE CLUB

227 East 56th Street/ 2nd & 3rd Avenues

☎ 753-2222

Rates: Cubicle $14, locker $10 ($2 extra from 4pm Friday to midnight Sunday)

Private club for members only, open 24 hours. On production of proper identification, out-of-towners may purchase a temporary membership for $10. Temporary members receive locker and changing-room privileges but may not rent private cubicles. Crowd is mostly white. After work patrons tend to be middle-aged, a younger crowd comes in later at night — after 9:00pm on weekdays and 11:00pm on weekends.

WALL STREET SAUNA

1 Maiden Lane

☎ 233-8900

Open Mon-Fri 11:00am-8:00pm; Sat noon-6:00pm

$10 (lockers only), $16 (for rooms)

Middle-aged to older Wall Street crowd. Busy during lunch hours and immediately after work. Many of the patrons here are making a quick stop after a busy day at the office before going home to their wives and families in the suburbs.

WEST SIDE CLUB

27 West 20th Street/ 6th & 5th Avenues/2nd Floor
☎ 691-2700
Open 24 hours.
Temporary membership $10 (proper photo id required).
Where else would you find the newest and most popular bathhouse in the city but in Chelsea? Same rates as for East Side Club.

MT. MORRIS BATHS

1944 Madison Avenue/ 124th & 125th Streets/in Harlem
☎ 534-9004
Open 24 hours, $15 (weekends), $12 (weekdays)
Predominantly Black clientele. Take cabs; you don't want to wander about after hours in this area.

BACKROOMS

What are the boys in the backroom doing? That depends on the year. Backrooms (or dark rooms as they are now sometimes called) disappeared in the early years of AIDS but made a comeback in the early 90s. Now political changes in the city have made them scarce again. Where boys get together in dark places in the bars and clubs, the sex may be safe, but the same cannot necessarily be said of the spaces, which are often small and badly ventilated, and have no emergency exits. Rarely comfortable or romantic, a quick trip to the backroom nevertheless eliminates the need to take home someone you'll regret having to face the next morning. And you can meet people from every walk of life in the anonymity of the backroom. I know of many friendships that have developed out of such chance encounters.

General tips for casual sexual activity in crowded places: BEWARE OF PICKPOCKETS. Dress down appropriately and don't carry a wallet. Keep your valuables in your shoe. Keep your wits about you and don't let anyone do anything that makes you feel uncomfortable.

MALE PORN CINEMAS/THEATERS/ VIDEOBOOTH STORES

With the clean-up of Times Square and the city's new zoning laws, zealous city politicians may succeed in driving porn theaters to the fringes of the island. Be aware that many establishments now employ annoying monitors who prevent people from even touching each other in public spaces.

Note: the videobooth stores/bookshops listed below also sell the latest gay male porn and bisexual videotapes, male pornography, dildos, lubricant and other sex toys. Since 1992, the sale of poppers has been illegal in the United States, but you often find them in some of these stores, described innocuously as "video head cleaner" or "liquid incense."

ALL MALE JEWEL THEATER

100 3rd Avenue/ 12th & 13th Streets
☎ 505-7320
Sun-Thu 10:00am-3:00am, $8
Fri-Sat 10:00am-5:00am, $10

Formerly the famous Bijou Theater (featured in David Leavitt's novel, *The Lost Language of Cranes*). There is no name on the door. You may have sex in the private booths in the basement, which you enter from behind the screen. Note: When it gets busy (particularly Sunday evenings) waiting for a empty booth can get very tedious.

BIJOU 82

82 East 4th Street/ 1st & 2nd Avenues
Thur-Sun 9:00pm-9:00am, $10

There is no name on the door and it maintains a very low profile and doesn't advertise in the gay press; but judging from its popularity, the Bijou 82 is no secret among the locals. There is plenty of space and areas for meeting people but sex is permitted only in the private booths.

CHRISTOPHER STREET BOOKSHOP

500 Hudson Street/ Christopher Street
☎ 463-0657
Admission $8 for private video booths in basement. Open 24 hours in the heart of Greenwich Village.

EROS MALE CINEMA

732 8th Avenue/ 45th Street
☎ 221-2450
The grungy porn cinema/strip joint has been given a makeover and now features shows presented by porn filmmaker Chi Chi LaRue. Movies are played in between the shows. No sex is permitted on the premises — you get hot and horny, meet someone else who is similarly aroused, but then you have to go somewhere private with him.

GAIETY

201 West 46th Street/ Broadway & 8th Avenue
☎ 221-8868
Sun-Thur 12:30pm-midnight; Fri & Sat 12:30pm-3:00am, $10
Tacky, but made chic by Madonna! The Gaiety burlesque dancers get their fifteen minutes of fame when they were featured with The Material Girl in her book, *Sex*. Sunday-Thursday: five strip shows a day featuring 6 or 7 dancers interspersed with porno movies. Fridays and Saturdays: No movies, marathon shows featuring 12 dancers with fifteen minute breaks. (Call for showtimes) The go-go boys are available for "private shows" afterwards at a nearby hotel for fees which can range from $100-$150, (negotiable, particularly on the slow nights). Note: Monitors now stop any attempts at sex between patrons in the auditorium.

HARMONY VIDEO

139 Christopher Street
☎ 366-9059
Open 24-hours
Private video booths in basement, magazines, videos and sexual paraphernalia upstairs.

LES HOMMES BOOKSHOP

217 West 80th Street/ Broadway & Amsterdam Avenue/2nd Floor
The only sex establishment on the Upper West Side, it gets very crowded after midnight. Screening room as well as booths.

UNICORN ALL MALE EROTICA

277C West 22nd Street/ 8th Avenue
☎ 924-2921
You won't be so surprised at the high quotient of cute boys you find in the Unicorn's booths when you realize this porn arcade is right next door to Barracuda, one of the hottest bars in Chelsea.

PRIVATE CLUBS

CELLBLOCK 28

(THE VAULT on straight nights)
28 10th Avenue/ 13th Street
☎ 255-6758
Sun-Thu 8:00pm-2:00am;
Fri-Sat 11pm-6am, $8 members;
$10 non-members

A subterranean cruise bar catering to the leather, levi and uniform crowd, but there is no mandatory dress code. The space includes a fully equipped dungeon for S/M action. Different themes and fetish nights.

J'S/THE HANGOUT

675 Hudson Street/ 14th Street
☎ 242-9292
Mon-Fri 9:00pm-8:00am; Sat & Sun opens at 4:00pm, $10

After hours club with basement lounge and backroom. J's is usually the last stop at the end of a long night of bar crawling. People don't usually get here until after 2:00 am.

THE MANHOLE

28 9th Avenue/ 14th Street
☎ 647-0063 or 24 hour infoline 647-1726
Mon-Wed 8pm-3am; Sun 5pm-11pm

After hours club in the meat-packing district; a venue for several J/O groups such as New York Jacks, The Renegades and Chestmen of America.

PARTIES

• The private parties which permit entry for "hard bodied hunks only" or "NYC's hottest men" are not listed here. There is nothing more obnoxious than a bouncer refusing you admission because he doesn't consider you attractive enough.

BLA-TINO

☎ 726-8406

Private safe sex parties for "athletic black and Latino guys in their 20s and 30s."

HANDS ON

28 10th Avenue/ 13th Street

Fridays 11pm-6pm, $10

Sundays 8pm-3am, $12

☎ 255-6758

Private sex parties. For information about special events write to be placed on mailing list to Hands On, 121 East 31st Street, Apt. 12D, New York, NY 10016.

HE'S GOTTA HAVE IT!

135 West 14th Street/ 6th & 7th Avenues/ 2nd Floor

☎ 677-3599

Admission $10

J/O parties for "men of all colors, sizes and ages," held on alternate Saturdays beginning at midnight. The organizers expressly state that they do not discriminate at the door, "because our community is already oppressed enough from the outside." A Big Dick Contest takes place at 2:00am. Check *HX* or call for the dates.

JACKS OF COLOR

☎ 827-5302

A safe sex club for people of color: Black, Caribbean, Latino, Asian, Pacific Islander, Native American, South Asian etc. Parties are usually held every first Saturday of the month at same location as "He's Gotta Have It!" (see above).

NYC UNCUT

135 West 14th Street, 2nd Floor

☎ 473-8078

Admission: $10

Bi-monthly parties for uncircumcised men and their admirers. "Kink, rubber, leather and raunch welcome." (Cut guys pay $5 more!)

NEW YORK JACKS

Monday nights at J'S/ THE HANGOUT

Sunday nights at MANHOLE (See PRIVATE CLUBS).

Nude, safe-sex J/O parties.

RENEGADES

P.O. Box 1457

New York, NY 10013

☎ 362-0347

Bondage parties held at J'S/THE HANGOUT and MANHOLE (see PRIVATE CLUBS).

SPANK ME HARD

135 West 14th Street

☎ 539-3549

Twice-monthly spanking party.

• Check the weekly listings in *HX* and *Next* for updates on the venues mentioned above.

HUSTLERS (RENT BOYS), MASSEURS & ESCORT/MODEL SERVICES

Now that ROUNDS, the city's oldest and best known hustler bar has been closed down, you may find boys discreetly plying their trade at THE TOWNHOUSE and perhaps at REGENTS on the East Side, JULIUS' in the Village and STELLA'S and CATS midtown. (See Bar listings)

In the wake of current police vigilance there is very little street trade. In any event, it's best to avoid hustlers you meet outside the bars. Individuals who advertise in the gay press are generally reliable, but be aware that like most personal ads the photos may be misleading.

Rates usually start at $40 in the seedier establishments. Prices increase according to your tastes and the services required and also the good looks and circumstances of the working boy.

A word of advice from a friend of mine who once supplemented his income by working in this business: treat the boys as professionals and without condescension. They like to be pampered, and if you take them to a nice dinner, they are likely to work harder! To avoid any embarrassment or unpleasantness later, don't leave the bar until you have confirmed the price and specified your wishes.

Transvestite hustlers, or Chicks with Dicks as they sometimes like to call themselves, usually hang out in the meat packing district of the West Village (Ninth Avenue/Gansevoort and Little West 12th Streets). Caution: this is a dangerous neighborhood, with gay bashers and vice cops. It's safer to look for them at the city's transvestite/transsexual bar, SALLY'S (See Bar listings).

MASSEURS: Legitimate practitioners mention that they are licensed in their advertisements. Otherwise, the service is most likely to be sex oriented.

ESCORT/MODEL SERVICES: Avoid those agencies which are sexually graphic in their advertisements. The more reliable ones have been in operation for a while and have maintained their quasi-legal status by being discreet. The better agencies screen their models as well as their clients and avoid conducting overtly sexual discussions on the telephone. Those which identify themselves as "gay owned and operated" are usually more trustworthy. The hourly rates for "models" at the better agencies start at about $150. Check your hotel's policy about visitors to avoid any embarrassment at the reception desk. Refer to ads in the *New York Native, Next* and *HX* for information.

PHONE SEX

A booming business in the age of AIDS. Some services provide erotic recordings, others connect you with other callers. For some gay men, just talking dirty on the phone is a turn on; others use the phone sex lines to meet men. Of course you never who know who you get until you meet him face to face. Read the ads carefully to see how much a call costs per minute — your phone bill after a little dirty talk can come as a rude shock to you or your host!

TEA-ROOMING (COTTAGING)

As celebrated by the New York poet Frank O'Hara in his poem "Homosexuality," subway toilets were very popular in the 50s, but such Joe Ortonesque activity ended when the city closed them all down.

There are toilets in certain public buildings which still have a reputation for being "tea-rooms" today, but listing would only focus an unnecessary spotlight on them. If you are tempted by the illicit thrills of "tea-rooming," be aware that most private businesses, department stores, hotels, etc., have security patrols. And do be considerate of the people (straight and gay) who need to use the toilet for its primary purpose. For what it is worth, I'll pass on a tip I got from a confirmed tea-room queen: if you plan to go into a stall with another person, bring along a shopping bag for one of you to stand inside. This way only one pair of feet will be visible under the door!

The New York City Police Department has become more aggressive about cracking down on public lewdness. Private agencies like the Port Authority police make routine sweeps through toilets. At all costs avoid the Grand Central, Penn Station, the Port Authority Bus Terminal or the World Trade Center "tea-rooms" — you may find yourself fondling a plain-clothes dick.

FETISHES & SPECIAL TASTES

If you have some special kink, it's more than likely someone has formed a group for it in New York. The following are some of the fetish groups in the city. (For leather and S/M groups refer also to the organizations listed in Chapter 7.)

CHESTMEN OF AMERICA
Meet at Cellblock 28 (see PRIVATE CLUBS).

CLUB FROTTAGE
For information send self-addressed envelope to P.O. Box 2119, Cathedral Station, New York, NY 10025.

GIRTH AND MIRTH CLUB
(see Chapter 7).

FOOT FRIENDS
☎ (718) 832-3952
Box 304, New York, NY 10014

HOT ASH
P.O. Box 20147, London Terrace Station, New York, NY 10011
☎ (718) 789-6147
For those interested in cigars. Meets at Cellblock 28.

NEW YORK BEARS

496A Hudson, Suite F4
New York, NY 10014

"For large, hairy men, their admirers and their chasers". Parties are held once a month at Cellblock 28. Send a self-addressed stamped envelope for information with a note stating that you are over 21.

METROBEARS NEW YORK

P.O. Box 1802
New York, NY 10185-1802
Email: NYBRUIN@aol.com

Sponsors events and activities for bears and bear-admirers in the tri-state area.

NEW YORK BONDAGE CLUB

P.O. Box 1189
New York, NY 10018

Meets at J's/The Hangout (see PRIVATE CLUBS).

NEW YORK STRAP & PADDLE ASSOCIATION

496 A Hudson Street, Suite F4
New York, NY 10014

Send a self-addressed stamped envelope for information (with a note stating that you are over 21) and refer Cellblock 28 listing.

THE RENEGADES

Box 1457, Canal Street Station
New York, NY 10013
☎ 362-0347

A "brotherhood of leathermen" organized to provide safe and consensual outlets for Leather, Rubber, Bondage S/M & fantasy play. Biweekly sex parties held at The Manhole and J's/The Hangout (See PRIVATE CLUBS).

UNCIRCUMCISED SOCIETY OF AMERICA,

P.O. Box 1052
New York, NY 10156
☎ 777-4208

A private nudist club for "Foreskins and their Friends." USA holds parties once or twice a month and publishes a newsletter. Write or call for more information.

WATER SPORTS CLUB

Write for information to NYPT
P.O. Box 783
New York, NY 10025-0783

For guys into golden showers (see glossary on following page if you need further explanation.)

GLOSSARY

basket — a well-stuffed crotch.

bottom — "passive" partner in anal intercourse.

buns — buttocks.

butch queen — a gay man who projects a stereotypical macho straight image.

chicken hawk — someone who is attracted to very young men.

chubby chaser — someone who likes fat men.

curry queen — finds South Asian men attractive.

dinge queen — a Caucasian attracted to Black men.

getting laid — having sex.

getting off, getting your rocks off — to come, to ejaculate.

hung — well endowed, genitally speaking.

j/o, jack off, jerk off, whack off — masturbate.

raunch — if you are into it, you've already checked out the listings above.

rice queen — finds East Asian men attractive.

rubber — condom.

scat — sexual activity involving feces.

schlong — you've guessed it. Yiddish for dick.

schtup — Yiddish for fuck.

size queen — someone who just will not be interested unless you can come up with more than seven inches!

sleaze queen — someone who has a large appetite for raunchy sex.

slut — someone who sleeps around.

snow queen — a person of color who is attracted to white guys.

top, top man — "active" partner in anal intercourse.

troll — the repulsive-looking man you don't want near you in a backroom.

twinkie — young, pretty boy, sometimes characterized as not very bright.

water sports — sexual activity involving urine, also called golden showers.

9: HEALTH

A national health care plan covering all Americans does not exist as of 1996. If you are visiting from overseas, you should consider taking out medical insurance for the trip. The 24-hour emergency rooms at all the city hospitals, however, are obliged to see anyone who is in need of critical medica attention.

• For specifically gay-related, sexually transmitted diseases:

COMMUNITY HEALTH PROJECT (CHP)

208 West 13th Street/7th Avenue
☎ 675-3559
Mon-Thur: 10:00am-9:00pm;
Fri: 10:00am-5:00pm
Walk-in Services for Sexually Transmitted Diseases (STDs):
Mon-Wed, 7:00pm-9:00pm (men and women);
Thur, 7:00pm-9:00pm (men only).
Fees: registration—$5;
Testing for syphilis and gonorrhoea (clap)—$15;
Medication—$10 (plus cost of medicine);
General Physical (by prior appointment)—$25.
Walk-in free counselling is also available. The CHP does not test for HIV.

AIDS HOTLINE

(operated by New York City):
☎ (718) 447-8200

GAY MEN'S HEALTH CRISIS

☎ AIDS Hotline: 807-6655.
Weekdays: 10:00am-9:00pm;
Sat: noon-3:00pm
Free walk-in counseling service (A-Team Counselling Service) available to everybody on a one-time basis Mon-Fri 11:00am-8:00pm (See also note in Chapter 7).

PEOPLE WITH AIDS COALITION

☎ Information: 647-1415;
Hotline: ☎ (800) 828-3280

SAFER SEX GUIDELINES

(adapted from safer sex information provided by Gay Men's Health Crisis)

You probably know this already, but give it a quick read anyway.

Whether you are HIV positive, HIV negative or Don't Know, *practice safer sex whenever you have sex.* Safer Sex will help protect you from HIV (Human Immunodeficiency Virus), the virus that causes AIDS. (If you are HIV positive, safer sex will protect you from getting exposed to HIV again and from other sexually transmitted diseases.) If you have sex with women, these guidelines still apply. The rule is: **Never let someone else's cum or blood get inside your body (and never let your cum or blood get inside anyone else's body).**

FUCKING: Whenever you're fucking or getting fucked, use a latex condom (rubber) with a water-based lubricant (lube). This is the only way to make fucking safer. For extra protection, pull out before cumming.

SUCKING: The biggest risk from sucking is getting cum in the mouth. Avoid oral sex immediately after brushing or flossing because your gums may be inflamed and may facilitate transmission of the virus. The only way to be totally safe is to lick only the shaft of the penis or to use a condom.

KISSING: There has never been a documented case of HIV being transmitted by kissing, but it is best to refrain if there are open sores in the mouth. Also, you may want to wait a few minutes after brushing or flossing for any potential breaks in the lining of the mouth to heal.

RIMMING (mouth to ass): A low risk for HIV transmission but a high risk for hepatitis and parasites. Rimming can be made safer by using a latex barrier between the mouth and the asshole. Either cut a condom up the side and unroll it, or use a dental dam (a square of latex used in dental surgery).

FISTING: Use latex surgical gloves when fisting. Don't insert the fist past the length of the glove. Keep finger nails trimmed and smooth. Use lots of water-based lube.

J/O (Jerking off) — masturbation alone, with a friend or in a group: Cum only on unbroken skin.

TOYS (dildos, butt plugs etc.): Don't share toys. Clean them with lots of soap and water after each use.

WATER SPORTS (and SCAT): Don't let anyone's piss or shit get inside your body.

DRUGS & ALCOHOL: You don't have to be a substance abuser for you to run the risk of impaired judgement. Keep your wits about you whenever you drink or take drugs. Don't go past your limits.

There's lots you can do that's safe and hot: massage, hugging, nipple-play, dry humping, fantasy, porn, sex talk. . . Use your imagination!

Knowing the safer sex guidelines is not enough. Once you have set your limits, you've got to be able to communicate them to your partners. Be assertive. Talk honestly and openly with your partners about your feelings. If you have set a boundary and you don't feel comfortable stepping over it, let him know in no uncertain terms.

CONDOMS: You can buy condoms at any drugstore (pharmacy), and most supermarkets or grocery stores, which you will find on practically every block in the city. *Trojan* and *Lifestyle* are popular brands. Many bars offer them to patrons free of charge. It's not uncommon to see someone grab a fistful as he walks proudly out into the night with his new catch. Sex clubs provide condoms and lubricant as well.

LUBRICANTS: Use only water-based lubricants and not Vaseline or other petroleum jellies. K-Y is a popular brand and is available at all drugstores and some supermarkets. The sex stores sell brands such as *ForPlay* and *Wet* which also contain Nonoxynol-9, a spermicide that might offer extra protection, but note that some people develop allergic reactions to it.

MEDICINE FOR CRABS: Lotions such as *Rid* and *A-200*are available over-the-counter at all drug stores.

Courtesy of the
estate of Keith Haring

10: CULTURE & ENTERTAINMENT

Great art may originate anywhere in the world but, as the jazz artists of the 20s used to say, when you play New York you play the Big Time. Since the 1850s, when the major publishing houses moved here from Boston, New York has been the cultural capital of America. Given Manhattan's unique concentration of world-famous art museums, the music, theater and dance venues, it's not without reason that most New Yorkers consider their city the cultural capital of the world as well.

CULTURAL EVENTS LISTINGS & INFORMATION

The "Arts and Leisure" section of Sunday's *New York Times*, and the "Weekend" section of the Friday *Times* carry comprehensive listings of the arts events in the city. For an alternative view of the arts scene pick up a free copy of the *Village Voice* or *New York Press*. *HX Magazine* and *Next* are good sources for gay or gay-popular cultural events in the city.

You will find listings of the week's cultural events in *The New Yorker* and *Time Out New York*, which along with *New York Magazine* also carry cinema and television program information. Another useful resource is *TheaterWeek*, which carries features, interviews, reviews and listings. In addition, browsing through any magazine store in the city you will find a plethora of papers and magazines reporting on the New York arts scene.

The League of American Theaters and *Playbill* publish the bi-weekly ***Broadway Theater Guide*** that includes a map of the Theater District and is available free at all Broadway theaters.

Two phonelines, THE BROADWAY SHOW LINE, ☎ 563-2929 and NYC/ON STAGE, ☎ 768-1818, give brief descriptions of the current Broadway and Off-Broadway shows, theater locations and ticket information, but be prepared to endure interminable computerized "menus" to get the information you want.

THEATER

BROADWAY

Theater and New York go hand in hand. The very name Broadway conjures glamour and spectacle, and symbolizes the pinnacle of American showbusiness. Seeing a Broadway show is a must on every visitor's list.

New York's **Theater District** has shifted several times over the past two centuries, moving uptown along Broadway from the Bowery as the city expanded north. A hundred years ago the first theaters opened in and around what is now called Times Square, establishing the Theater District as we know it today — the twelve blocks between 41st and 53rd Streets bounded by 6th and 9th Avenues. In 1901, an advertising executive envisioned the commercial possibilities of the area lit up with electric billboards and theater marquees and coined the name **"Great White Way"** for the strip of Broadway that runs through the theater district. The term Broadway is generally applied to the shows which play in those theaters, usually seating 500 or more, located in the theater district. In the wake of a public outcry in the early 1980s, when developers tore down two ornately decorated "jewel box" Broadway playhouses to make way for a tourist hotel, most of the Broadway houses are now designated New York City landmarks. (In the wake of the revitalization of Times Square, several defunct theaters on 42nd

Street are now being restored and refurbished.) Don't be confused by the fact that only four of the "Broadway theaters" are actually situated on Broadway; the rest are located on the nearby side streets.

The American musical is an artform that was created and perfected on Broadway: *Anything Goes, Porgy and Bess, Oklahoma!, Guys and Dolls, West Side Story, My Fair Lady, Hello Dolly!, Gypsy, Hair, Sweeney Todd,* and *A Chorus Line* — need one say more? Broadway musical fans should not miss the permanent exhibition "Broadway: 125 Years of Musical Theater" at the Museum of the City of New York (see Museums below) for the largest collection of costumes and set models in the world.

Unlike most European countries the U.S. does not have a government subsidized national theater. Broadway theater is free market economics at work, which unfortunately leaves too little room for risk-taking and innovation. Broadway once meant plays by Eugene O'Neill, Clifford Odets, Arthur Miller and Tennessee Williams. In today's commercial environment, it has become a repository for enormous, spectacle-driven musicals, bland comedies and sure-fire revivals targeted at very wide audiences. Happily, there are exceptions. Tony Kushner's greatly acclaimed *Angels in America* (a theatrically daring, two-part epic subtitled *"A Gay Fantasia on National Themes,"*) won both the 1993 and 1994 Tony awards (Broadway's highest accolade) for Best Play.

Julie Andrews in the role of 'Victor' in VICTOR/VICTORIA
photo copyright © Francesco Scavullo

OFF-BROADWAY AND RESIDENT THEATER COMPANIES

The Off-Broadway movement emerged as an economic and artistic alternative to Broadway with the 1952 production of Tennessee Williams' *Summer and Smoke* in Greenwich Village. Subscriber-funded Off-Broadway resident companies are able to take greater risks than commercial producers on Broadway. These days, even new plays by established playwrights like Arthur Miller, Terrence McNally, Sam Shepard, David Mamet, Marsha Norman, and Lanford Wilson are more likely to open Off-Broadway.

Check out the work of the following New York resident companies:

CIRCLE REPERTORY COMPANY

99 Seventh Avenue South
Greenwich Village
☎ 924-7100

Circle Rep has produced most of Lanford Wilson's plays and, Larry Kramer's *The Destiny of Me*.

LINCOLN CENTER THEATER

150 West 65th Street
☎ 239-6200

The company produces at the Vivian Beaumont Theater (technically a Broadway house) where *Carousel* was revived, on Broadway (Edward Albee's *A Delicate Balance*) and the smaller Mizti Newhouse Theater, where John Guare's *Six Degrees of Separation* premiered.

MANHATTAN THEATER CLUB

at City Center, 131 W 55th Street/ 6th & 7th Avenues
☎ 581-1212

MTC has produced Terrence McNally's recent hits, *The Lisbon Traviata* and *Love! Valour! Compassion!* and highly successful revivals of Joe Orton's *What the Butler Saw* and *Loot*.

PLAYWRIGHTS HORIZONS

416 West 42nd Street/ 9th & 10th Avenues
☎ 279-4200

Stephen Sondheim's *Sunday in the Park with George* and William Finn's *Falsettos* first saw the light of day at this theater.

ROUNDABOUT THEATER
1530 Broadway/ at 45th Street
☎ 869-8400
Noted for recent revivals of *The Night of the Iguana*, *Company*, and *She Loves Me*, Roundabout offers subscribers a gay singles night for each of their productions.

THE NEW YORK SHAKE-SPEARE FESTIVAL
at the JOSEPH PAPP PUBLIC THEATER
475 Lafayette Street
☎ 260-2400
NYSF produced Larry Kramer's *The Normal Heart* and *A Chorus Line*.

Well-known and forgotten classics are presented on Broadway by the **National Actors Theater**, ☎ 239-6280, and Off-Broadway by the **Classic Theater Company** (CSC), ☎ 677-4210, the **Pearl Theater Company** ☎ 645-7708 and the **Cocteau Repertory Company** ☎ 677-0060. The **York Theater Company**, ☎ 534-5366, has scored great successes in the past with revivals of Sondheim's *Pacific Overtures* and *Sweeney Todd*, and *Merrily We Roll Along*. **New York Theater Workshop**, 79 East 4th Street, ☎ 302-6989 has established a reputation for quality work and recently produced the Pulitzer Prize-winning Broadway musical *Rent*; and **En Garde Arts**, ☎ 941-9793 presents "site-specific" theater at unusual venues. In a class all of its own is **The Ridiculous Theater Company** where the gloriously "ridiculous" tradition created by the late Charles Ludlum is carried on by his lover and collaborator Everett Quinton. Black artists are represented at **The Federal Theater Project**, Asian artists have a platform at **Pan Asian Repertory**, ☎ 245-2660, and Latino artists at **Intar Hispanic Arts Center**, ☎ 695-6551 and **Repertorio Espanol** ☎ 889-2850. You can catch young actors at the beginning of the careers at the **Julliard School**, 70 Lincoln Plaza, ☎ 769-7406, where you may see the next Kevin Kline or William Hurt.

The Brooklyn Academy of Music, 30 Lafayette Avenue, Brooklyn, ☎ (718) 636-4100, often sponsors the work of international theater artists of the caliber of Peter Brook, Ingmar Bergman and Ariane Mnouchkine, and presents in the fall, the annual NEXT WAVE FESTIVAL, New York's most popular avant-garde performance series.

OFF-OFF BROADWAY

Outside of Broadway and Off-Broadway you can experience the full range of experimental drama, performance art and mixed media presentations — some of it gay-themed. The Off-Off Broadway movement evolved in the 1960s from the politically and sexually daring work spearheaded by New York's premier avant-garde institution, **La Mama Experimental Theater Company (La Mama Etc)**, 74A East 4th Street, ☎ 475-7710. The other Off-Off Broadway theaters in the city include: **Dixon Place**, 258 the Bowery (south of Houston Street), ☎ 219-3088; **Franklin Furnace**, 112 Franklin Street, ☎ 925-4671; **Here**, 145 Avenue of the Americas (at Spring Street), ☎ 647-0202; **The Kitchen**, 512 West 19th Street, ☎ 255-5793; **P.S. 122**, 150 1st Avenue at 9th Street, ☎ 477-5288; **Mabou Mines** ☎ 473-0559; **The Performance Garage (The Wooster Group)**, 33 Wooster Street, ☎ 966-3651; and **Theater for a New City**, 155 1st Avenue at 10th Street, ☎ 254-1109.

FREE SHAKESPEARE IN THE PARK

In July and August the New York Shakespeare Festival continues an annual tradition of free plays by Shakespeare and others, in Central Park's open-air Delacorte Theater (near West 80th Street). The quality of the productions can vary greatly, but it's hard to beat the atmosphere of theater under the stars with the Park's Belvedere Castle and lake serving as a backdrop. In addition, the productions often feature many well-known movie stars. Tickets are given out free on the day of the show starting at 1:00pm at the Delacorte Theater and are also available from 1:00pm-3:00pm from the Joseph Papp Public Theater, ☎ 861-7277 (in the summer only) or 598-7100 for details.

GAY THEATER

There are many prominent American playwrights who are openly gay or lesbian currently writing for the New York stage — Edward Albee, Jon Robin Baitz, Tony Kushner, Craig Lucas, Terrence McNally, Paul Rudnick, Paula Vogel, Lanford Wilson, to name a few. The recent success of *Angels in America, Jeffrey, Falsettos* and *The Destiny of Me* has shown that gay-themed work can successfully cross-over to non-gay audiences. Though traditionally associated with gay entertainment, drag and camp also attracts wide audiences in New York. In this context try and catch the work of **The Ridiculous Theater Company**; **Lypsinka** (John Epperson), who has elevated lip-synching to a sublime art-form; and **Charles Busch** who made a name with his smash productions of *Vampire Lesbians of Sodom, Psycho Beach Party*, and *The Lady in Question*. Drag superstar **RuPaul**, whose motto is "You are born naked, and the rest is drag," is one of the many New York drag divas who perform at Wigstock, the annual open-air drag festival held in September.

New York's gay and lesbian theater companies are: **The Glines,** ☎ 354-8899 (producers of *Torch Song Trilogy*); **Wings Theater**, in the Archive Building, 154 Christopher Street, ☎ 627-2961; **The Vortex Theater Co.** ☎ 206-1764; **3 Dollar Bill Theater** ☎ 477-5171, which together with **Dixon Place** presents HOT, an annual "Celebration of Queer Culture" in June.

NOTES TO THEATERGOERS

Most theaters are dark either Sundays or Mondays (there are a few exceptions). Broadway houses are dark on Sunday evenings, while some Off-Broadway shows have Sunday evening performances. Matinees are Wednesdays, Saturdays and Sundays. Your theater ticket entitles you to a free program, *Playbill* or *Stagebill*. You are not expected to tip the ushers.

The theater industry's two major ticket agencies (booking by phone via credit card) are TELE-CHARGE ☎ 239-6200 or (800) 233-3123 ($4.50 service charge per ticket) and TICKETMASTER ☎ 307-4100 ($5 service charge per ticket). If you go to the theater box-office in person, you avoid the excessive service charges and get to choose the seat locations yourself. For tickets and information about Theater Row (on 42nd Street between 9th & 10th Avenues) shows call TICKET CENTRAL ☎ 279-4200 (1:00pm-8:00pm).

Ticket prices are steep. At this writing the top rate for a Broadway musical is $75, and $60 for a Broadway play. Occasionally you can buy standing room tickets or student tickets ($15-20), which are generally sold only on the day of the show. Off-Broadway rates are lower, usually between $35-$45. Avoid scalpers. You may get ripped off; selling tickets for a profit is against the law. Check the publications listed at the beginning of this chapter for information on the many free cultural events in New York, particularly during the summer.

Discount Theater Tickets

Reduced theater tickets for both Broadway and Off-Broadway shows are available from TKTS, a service operated by the Theater Development Fund. ☎ 768-1818 for recorded information about their services.

There are two TKTS locations in Manhattan: the more popular orange and white booth situated midtown at 47th Street and Broadway, and a booth at Two World Trade Center, Mezzanine level, downtown. Reduced tickets, discounted 25% or 50% depending on the show (plus a $2.50 service charge per ticket), may be purchased on the day of the performance between 3:00pm and 8:00pm Mon-Sat. Wednesday and Saturday matinees tickets are sold from 10:00am to 2:00pm and for all Sunday performances from noon till closing (about 7:00pm).

Only cash or travellers checks accepted. No credit cards. Lines form at the TKTS booth as early as two or three hours before the tickets go on sale for the evening performances, but if you go between 6:30pm or 7:00pm you can sometimes get tickets (with good locations) to choice shows. The World Trade Center booth is open 11:00am-5:30pm Mon-Fri and from 1:30pm on Saturdays. Matinee tickets are sold a day in advance of the performance.

At several bookstores around town and the NYC Visitors Convention Bureau you can pick up Discount Coupons ("Twofers" — Two-for-One), which enable you to buy tickets at slightly more than 50% of the full price directly at the box office.

For the past few years Off-Broadway theaters have designated March and April as OFF-BROADWAY MONTH/s. Keep your eye out for special discount offers during that period.

DANCE

Just as theater-lovers believe that New York is the theater capital of the world, dance enthusiasts consider the Big Apple the world capital of ballet and modern dance. The **New York City Ballet**, founded in 1948, enjoys a world class reputation. The troupe performs at the **New York State Theater** in Lincoln Center, 63rd Street and Columbus Avenue, ☎ 870-5570, for a season that runs from November through February. Their production of *The Nutcracker* is a winter holiday tradition. NYCB's equally renowned rival ballet company, **American Ballet Theater** performs from April through June at the **Metropolitan Opera House**, which is situated at right angles to the State Theater in the Lincoln Center complex, ☎ 362-6000.

Some of the other best known and popular dance companies that work in New York are listed below under the theaters at which they usually perform. Keep an eye out for the work of New York's best known openly gay choreographers: **Bill T. Jones** (Bill T. Jones/Arnie Zane Company), and **Mark Morris** (Mark Morris Dance Group).

Outside of the Lincoln Center, there are four main spaces for dance in New York:

CITY CENTER THEATER

West 55th Street/ 6th & 7th Avenues)
☎ 581-7907
Built as a Masonic temple in 1924 by the Shriners, and called The Mecca after its Moorish architecture, it was saved from demolition and turned into a theater in 1943. Once the home of both the Metropolitan Opera and New York City Ballet, it now hosts many dance companies from around the world as well as many New York modern dance companies including: **Alvin Ailey American Dance Company, Dance Theater of Harlem, Eric Hawkins Dance Company, The Joffrey Ballet, Martha Graham Dance Company, Merce Cunningham Dance Company, Paul Taylor Dance Company** and **Twyla Tharp**.

JOYCE THEATER

175 Eighth Avenue/ West 19th Street
☎ 242-0800
This Art Moderne theater is the venue for dance companies not big enough for the City Center and which have outgrown the smaller spaces. The Joyce is the permanent home of the **Feld Ballet** and regularly hosts companies such as **Ballet Hispanico, David Parsons Company, Garth Fagan Bucket Company, Lar Lubovitch Dance Company, Limon Dance Company, Nikolais and Murray Dance Company** and **Pilobolus**.

DANCE THEATER WORKSHOP

219 West 19th Street
☎ 691-6500
The principal space for avant garde and experimental dance in the city.

BROOKLYN ACADEMY OF MUSIC

(see under THEATER)
This is often a venue for visiting dance companies.

MUSIC

CLASSICAL MUSIC

The **Lincoln Center** is one of the prime venues for classical music in New York. The city's most prestigious orchestra, the **New York Philharmonic**, ☎ 875-5656, now over 150 years old, performs at **Avery Fisher Hall**, ☎ 875-5030 (65th Street and Broadway in Lincoln Center). The season runs from September through June. Whenever soloists and conductors are amenable, the general public may attend morning rehearsals for $10.

Check the newspaper listings for details of New York Philharmonic (and Metropolitan Opera) free summer events in the city parks, and free concerts in Lincoln Center.

Alice Tully Hall, situated at 66th Street and Broadway, ☎ 875-5050, is also a part of the Lincoln Center complex and hosts classical groups from all over the world, including **New York's Chamber Music Society of Lincoln Center** and the **Guarneri Quartet**.

New York City's oldest and the most famous auditorium is **Carnegie Hall**, Seventh Avenue at 57th Street, ☎ 247-7800, which was built by multi-millionaire Andrew Carnegie in 1891. Since its opening with a gala concert conducted by Tchaikovsky, maestros such as Mahler, Toscanni and Stokowski have conducted at Carnegie Hall. In 1943 a young Leonard Bernstein made his spectacular debut here. Ask a New Yorker how you get to Carnegie Hall and you'll get the oft-repeated wisecrack, "Practice, practice, practice!" Indeed, Carnegie Hall represents the pinnacle to which all performers, not just classical artists, aspire. Duke Ellington, the Beatles and Liza Minnelli have all performed here. **The Gay Men's Chorus** hold their regular concert series in this famed auditorium.

Other venues for classical music in the city include: **The Brooklyn Academy of Music**, 30 Lafayette Avenue, ☎ (718) 636-4100; **Merkin Concert Hall**, 129 West 67th Street, ☎ 362-8719; **The 92nd Street Y**, at Lexington Avenue, ☎ 415-5440, home to the **New York Chamber Symphony**; **Symphony Space**, Broadway at 95th Street, ☎ 864-5400, which presents classical and ethnic music programs, and the **Town Hall**, 123 West 43rd Street (Broadway & 6th Avenue), ☎ 840-2824. At the Paul Recital Hall of **Julliard School** in the Lincoln Center complex, ☎ 769-7406, you can attend low priced student recitals and faculty performances.

OPERA

Like the two major ballet companies, New York's two premier opera companies, the Metropolitan Opera Company and The New York City Opera, perform at Lincoln Center. **The Metropolitan Opera Company**, ☎ 362-6000, is the grander of the two companies. The lobby of the Metropolitan Opera House (at West 64th Street) is adorned with two murals by Marc Chagall (covered during the day) and is dominated by an impressive staircase and grand chandeliers. The drama begins even before the curtain goes up on the opulent productions as the huge chandeliers rise majestically to the roof of the 3,800 seat auditorium. The Met boasts an international roster of stars which include Placido Domingo, Luciano Pavarotti, Theresa Stratas and Cecilia Bartolli. The Met season runs from mid-September to April. **The New York City Opera**, ☎ 870-5570, performs from July through November at the adjacent New York State Theater (at West 63rd Street). Its repertoire includes classic and contemporary work, as well as operettas and Broadway musicals. For backstage tours of the Lincoln Center ☎ 875-5351. Outside Lincoln Center, subscribers often sell their unused

METROPOLITAN OPERA HOUSE photo copyright © Stephen DiMenna

seats to opera, dance and classical music performances at reduced prices on the evening of the show.

Other opera companies in New York include: **Amato Opera** which performs a classical repertoire, on a much smaller scale and infinitely smaller budgets than the Met, from September through May in their tiny East Village space at 319 Bowery at 2nd Street, ☎ 228-8200; **The New York Gilbert and Sullivan Players,** ☎ 769-1000 who perform in the city during Christmas and New Year at Symphony Space, and **Opera Ebony,** ☎ 874-7245, a Black company which performs September through June.

JAZZ

New York Jazz first thrived in Harlem, which was a magnet for Black artists during the Harlem Renaissance of the 1920s and 30s. In the mid 1930s, just after Prohibition, the city's most famous jazz clubs sprang up on West 52nd Street between 5th and 6th Avenues. But great clubs of *Swing Street*, as it came to be called, closed down in the early 1950s, to be replaced by office blocks. New York jazz clubs are now scattered throughout the city, with a large concentration in Greenwich Village. Listed below are a few clubs, some of which are landmarks in jazz history.

Clubs in HARLEM include: **The Cotton Club**, 666 West 125th Street at Broadway, ☎ 663-7980, whose heyday was from 1923-1935 when it was located at 142nd Street between Lenox and Fifth Avenues. Josephine Baker, Cab Calloway, Duke Ellington, and Lena Horne all headlined here. It is currently a venue for blues, jazz and gospel and offers shows with dinner and brunch. **Showman's Cafe**, 2321 Eighth Avenue (at 125th Street), ☎ 864-8941, a historic jazz supper club whose current location is around the corner from its original space, which was destroyed by a fire.

Situated on the UPPER WEST SIDE is **Birdland** at 2745 Broadway (West 105th Street), ☎ 749-2228, a noted jazz supper club which takes its name from the original 52nd Street club made famous by Charlie Parker.

Clubs in GREENWICH VILLAGE: **The Blue Note**, 131 West Third Street (at 6th Avenue), ☎ 475-8592; **Bradley's**, 70 University Place (south of 11th Street), ☎ 473-9700; **Sweet Basil**, 88 Seventh Avenue South (at Bleecker Street), ☎ 242-1785; and **The Village Vanguard**, 178 Seventh Avenue (at Perry Street), ☎ 255-4037, the oldest jazz club in New York, where today's performers follow in the footsteps of John Coltrane, Thelonius Monk, Miles Davis, Dexter Gordon and Lee Konitz.

You may also want to visit **Fat Tuesday's**, 190 Third Avenue (at 17th Street), ☎ 533-7902; **The Knitting Factory**, 47 East Houston Street (between Mott and Mulberry Streets), ☎ 219-3055, which specializes in cutting edge jazz and new music as created by the likes of John Zorn and Elliott Sharp. Also worth a trip is **S.O.B.'s**, 204 Varrick Street at West Houston, ☎ 243-4940 (that's Sounds of Brazil, by the way) for funky Afro-Caribbean music.

Jazz enthusiasts should not miss the **JVC Jazz Festival**, which is held every June — for details write c/o P. O. Box 1169, New York, New York 10023, or ☎ 787-2020; and the Greenwich **Village Jazz Festival** which is held in the months of August and September.

FOLK, ROCK, OTHER

The heart of the folk movement was the now defunct FOLK CITY on West Third Street, where Bob Dylan and Arlo Guthrie began their careers, and the many clubs on Bleecker Street in Greenwich Village. Check out **CBGBs** at 315 Bowery, ☎ 982-4052. The full name "CBGB and OMFUG", stands for "Country, BlueGrass and Blues and Other Music for Uplifting Gormandizers," but this dark cave, which was the center of punk in the 1970s and the launching pad for bands like Blondie, Talking Heads and Living Color, is now one of the major venues for Alternate Music in the city.

For up to date information on current rock music events refer the Village Voice and the flyers and posters at the city's premier record shops TOWER RECORDS, HMV RECORDS and VIRGIN MEGASTORE.

NEW YORK ENTERTAINMENT LANDMARKS

The following New York locations are part of American show-biz and entertainment history:

The **Apollo Theater**, 253 West 125th Street (7th & 8th Avenues), ☎ 864-0372, is Harlem's world-famous showcase for talent which, since 1934, has featured the greatest names in Black entertainment: Billie Holiday, Duke Ellington, Count Basie, Aretha Franklin, Sammy Davis, Jr., Miles Davis, Gladys Knight and the Pips, and Bessie Smith to name just a few. The legendary Amateur Night still takes place on Wednesdays.

A visit to **Radio City Music Hall**, 1260 Avenue of the Americas at 50th Street, ☎ 247-4777, is a unique theatrical experience. The Art Deco palace opened as a variety house in 1932, operated by the great showman Samuel "Roxy" Rothafel. The following year it became the country's most prestigious movie house hosting the premieres of, among others, *King Kong*, *Top Hat* and *An American in Paris*. Today it is used for musical spectaculars like the Easter and Christmas shows with the Rockettes, Radio City's famous precision dancers; for special movie events such as the premiere of the restored *A Star is Born*; and concerts by pop personalities and groups from the B52s to Bette Midler. The movie version of Evita starring Madonna premieres here in the fall of 1996. ☎ 632-4041 for information about tours of the building.

Roseland, 239 West 52nd Street (Broadway & 8th Avenue), ☎ 247-0200, the legendary ballroom with one of the biggest dance floors in New York, is now mostly a place for old-timers with nostalgic memories, but occasionally hosts gay events such as the Saint-at-Large parties.

CABARET

The following are some of the popular cabaret spots in Manhattan, many of which present gay or gay-friendly artists: **Algonquin (The Oak Room)**, 59 West 44th Street (5th & Madison Avenues), romantic in a Harry Connick Jr. kind of way, ☎ 840-6800; **The Ballroom**, 253 West 28th Street at 8th Avenue, ☎ 244-3005, the home of divas — Peggy Lee, Eartha Kitt, Charles Pierce, Lypsinka and Charles Busch; **Don't Tell Mama**, 343 West 46th Street (between 8th and 9th Avenues), ☎ 757-0788, a piano bar and cabaret in the heart of the theater district; **Duplex**, 61 Christopher Street (at Seventh Avenue) ☎ 255-5438; **Eighty Eights**, 238 West 10th Street, ☎ 924-0088, the most adventurous cabaret spot in New York; **55 Grove Street Cabaret at Rose's Turn**, ☎ 366-5438; **Rainbow and Stars**, 30 Rockefeller Plaza at Fifth Avenue, on the 65th floor, ☎ 632-5000, a great view but you pay a high price for it; and **The Triad**, 158 West 72nd Street (at Broadway), ☎ 595-7400.

GAY MUSIC GROUPS

THE FLIRTATIONS

☎ (508) 487-0873
Email: Flirts@wn.net
Website: http://www.ptownlib.com/users/ptown/flirt.html

Founded in 1987 and advertised as "the world's most famous openly gay politically aware a capella doo-wop singing group".

LAVENDER LIGHT: The Black and People of Color Lesbian and Gay Gospel Choir

70A Greenwich Avenue
Suite 315, New York, NY 10011
☎ 714-7072

Founded in 1985, Lavender Light gives two concerts a year at Tribeca Performing Arts Center (Borough of Manhattan Community College, 199 Chambers Street) as well as performances at other venues in the city.

NEW YORK CITY GAY MEN'S CHORUS

55 Christopher Street
New York, NY 10014
☎ 924-7770; Fax: 924-6660

The best known and most popular gay music group in the city, founded in 1980. The Chorus performs Broadway show tunes, film music, opera, as well as commissioned original works. They hold three concerts a year at Carnegie Hall: one in December featuring traditional holiday music, a Pops Concert in March and a Gay Pride Concert during Pride Week in June.

OUTMUSIC

P.O. Box 1575
New York, NY 10013
☎ 330-9197

Outmusic was formed in 1990 to create opportunities for lesbian and gay composers, lyricists and musical performers. The group holds an annual Outmusic Festival and usually meets on the third Sunday of each month at the Lesbian and Gay Community Center and hosts open mikes concerts on the first Monday of every month also at the Center.

MUSEUMS & ART GALLERIES

New York has been famous for its museums and galleries since the late 1800s. Some originating as private collections by multi-millionaires and others established to reflect the cultural diversity of New York, there are over 150 museums and over 400 galleries in the city's five boroughs. The 20-block stretch on upper 5th Avenue between 83rd and 103rd Streets is known as "MUSEUM MILE".

New Yorkers are inveterate museum-goers and will line up for blocks to see exhibitions at the Metropolitan and at the Museum of Modern Art.

The listings below represent some of New York's best known and best loved art, science and cultural museums. For more information consult Betty Ross' excellent guide titled *New York City Museums* and the periodical *Museums New York* available at newstands. Please check with the individual institutions to confirm opening hours and for details of tours; make note when reduced or free admission is offered. If you are on strict budget, take advantage of the fact that some institutions list suggested admission prices only.

AMERICAN MUSEUM OF NATURAL HISTORY

Central Park West at West 79th Street

☎ 769-5000, 769-5100 (recording)

Enter through its Central Park West entrance and you confront the immense Barosaurus skeleton in the Theodore Roosevelt Memorial Wing. One the big attractions is the famed dinosaur collection. Visit the Morgan Memorial Hall of Gems which displays the spectacular 563 carat Star of India sapphire (acquired in Sri Lanka by J.P. Morgan) and the Princess Topaz from Brazil, the world's largest cut gem. At the museum's NATUREMAX FILM THEATER (separate admission required) science films are screened on a mammoth screen. Also part of the museum is the HAYDEN PLANETARIUM (West 81st Street).

THE BROOKLYN MUSEUM

200 Eastern Parkway/
at Washington Avenue,
Prospect Heights
☎ (718) 638-5000
Wed-Sun 10:00am-5:00pm;
Suggested admission $4

An impressive Beaux Arts building houses one of America's oldest art collections: the largest collection of Egyptian antiquities outside of Egypt and the British Museum; Greek, Roman, Coptic and Nubian art; rare examples of Primitive and African art; antique Chinese porcelains and a noteworthy collection of European and American sculpture and painting. Brooklyn Museum's sculpture garden is a repository for architectural ornaments, columns and stonework rescued in the wake of New York's passion from demolition, including elements from the late lamented Penn Station (built by museum's architects, McKim, Mead & White). The Brooklyn Museum is not difficult to get to: take the 2 or the 3 subway to the Eastern Parkway-Brooklyn Museum stop.

THE CLOISTERS

Fort Tryon Park, West 190th
Street and Fort Washington
Avenue
☎ 923-3700,
Tue-Sun 9:30am-5:15pm (earlier in
the winter) and closed Mondays.
Admission $6 (also covers
Metropolitan Museum of Art) Take
the M4 bus which drops you off at
the door to the museum.

The Cloisters houses the Metropolitan Museum of Art's Medieval Collection and is located in one of New York's most beautiful locations, on a wooded hilltop near the northernmost tip of Manhattan. With covered walkways and open courtyards, the museum was built with elements from authentic medieval monasteries, churches, and chapels brought back from Europe by its benefactor, John D. Rockefeller, Jr. Its highlights are the celebrated Unicorn Tapestries (circa 1500) and the enclosed herb garden planted with the same species represented in the tapestries.

COOPER-HEWITT MUSEUM

National Museum of Design, Smithsonian Institute

2 East 91st Street/ 5th Avenue
☎ 860-6868,
Tue 10:00am-9:00pm, Wed-Sat
10:00am-5:00pm; Sun noon-
5:00pm. Closed Mon, Admission $3
(Free on Tuesdays 5:00pm-
9:00pm).

A branch of the Smithsonian Institution devoted to past and contemporary international design, the Cooper Hewitt features prints, drawings, furniture, wallpaper, textiles, jewelry, ceramics, glass, metalwork and even buttons and Christmas Tree ornaments. It is housed in the mansion of 19th century industrialist Andrew Carnegie. Closed till September 1996.

FORBES MAGAZINE GALLERIES

62 Fifth Avenue
☎ 206-5549
Tue-Sat 10:00am-4:00pm; Closed Sun and Mon. Admission Free

An eclectic display of toys, objets d'art and presidential memorabilia collected by the late business tycoon Malcolm Forbes, publisher of the eponymous biweekly business magazine. Forbes collected over 500 toy boats, thousands of toy soldiers and the work of Peter Carl Fabergé (including 12 Imperial Easter eggs, said to be rivalled only by Queen Elizabeth II's collection). The now defunct gay publication *OutWeek* fuelled the debate on the ethics of "outing" public personalities when it revealed Forbes' homosexuality after he died in 1991.

FRICK COLLECTION

1 East 70th Street/ 5th Avenue
☎ 288-0700
Tue-Sat 10:00am-6:00pm;
Sun 1:00pm-6:00pm; Closed Mon.
Admission $3

Originally amassed by steel magnate Henry Clay Frick and housed in what was his mansion, the collection includes works by Bellini, Vermeer, Rembrandt, El Greco; portraits by Holbein and landscapes by Constable and Turner; 18th century French furniture; porcelains from the K'ang Hsi and Ch'ien Lung dynasties and an impressive array of Renaissance bronze sculpture. This is one of the most important private collections ever assembled.

METROPOLITAN MUSEUM OF ART

Fifth Avenue/ at East 82nd Street
☎ 879-5500, 535-7710 (recording
Tue-Thur, Sun 9:30am-5:15pm;
Fri-Sat 9:30am-8:45pm;
Closed Mon. Admission $6

Founded in 1870, the Metropolitan is the crown jewel of New York museums. Don't miss the Egyptian wing, which houses the ancient Temple of Dendur (c.15 BC) given by the Egyptian government in 1965 after flooding from the Aswan Dam along the Nile threatened to submerge the impressive monument. Also noteworthy are the collections of Islamic art, Sumerian and Assyrian archeological treasures, and an impressive Primitiv Art collection which includes som of the largest phalloi you'll eve see! The American wing contain an exemplary collection of Americana: painting, sculpture, furniture Tiffany glass, Colonial pewter, etc The Metropolitan's collection c European masterpieces includ Old Masters, Impressionists an Post-Impressionists: Rembrandt Vermeer, Botticelli, Brueghel Caravaggio, El Greco, Gaugin Goya, Hieronymous Bosch et a Extremely popular are the fashio history exhibitions from the Metropolitan's Costume Institute; i the past these have included th clothing of Indian princes and a underwear collection featurin Jean-Paul Gaultier's corsets fo Madonna.

MUSEUM OF MODERN ART (MoMA)

11 West 53rd Street/ 5th & 6th Avenues
☎ 708-9480
Fri-Tue 11:00am-6:00pm;
Thur 11:00am-9:00pm; Closed Wed
Admission $7 (voluntary contribution Thur 5:00pm-9:00pm)

MoMA (pronounce it as one word), which opened just days after the stock market crash in November 1929, is one of the most popular cultural institutions in New York, and contains the world's best collection of 20th century art. The painting and sculpture collection features Post-Impressionist masterpieces by Van Gogh and Monet and works of the modernists such as Picasso, Surrealists such as Dali, as well as extensive collections of abstract and popular art and just about every 20th century artistic movement. The museum also houses a large photography installation and has floors devoted to architecture, design and drawing. The Museum's Film department screens movies daily (free for the price of admission to the museum). In the Museum's Sculpture Garden, New Yorkers can enjoy moments of tranquility amidst works by Picasso, Rodin and Oldenburg.

PIERPONT MORGAN LIBRARY

29 East 36th Street/ at Madison Avenue
☎ 685-0008
Tue-Sat 10:30am-5:00pm;
Sun 1:00-5:00pm; Closed Mon
Admission: Suggested donation $3

A world famous library containing treasured medieval and Renaissance manuscripts; a Gutenberg Bible; one of the original twenty-two copies of the Declaration of Independence; drawings and prints by Dürer, Michelangelo, Rembrandt, etc.; and autographed scores by Bach, Mozart, Beethoven, Stravinsky, and Gilbert & Sullivan.

SOLOMON R. GUGGENHEIM MUSEUM

1071 Fifth Avenue at 88th Street
☎ 360-3500, 423-3500 (recording)
Fri-Wed 10:00am-8:00pm;
Closed Thur. Admission $7 (pay as you wish Tue 5:00pm-8:00pm)

What began as a private collection by mining tycoon Solomon Guggenheim is contained in a New York City landmark, designed by Frank Lloyd Wright. The spiral-shaped building, said to be inspired by the ziggurats of ancient Babylon, enables the visitor to view the paintings and sculpture from different vantage points. The best way to see the collection is to wind your way up the ramp which curves up to the 100 foot-high dome. The museum's holdings include works by Klee, Chagall,

Kandinsky, Picasso, Brancusi, Braque, Cezanne, Gaugin, Manet and Van Gogh.

The Guggenheim's downtown branch is located in SoHo at 575 Broadway at Prince Street, Admission $5.

WHITNEY MUSEUM OF AMERICAN ART

945 Madison Avenue/ at 75th Street
☎ 570-3600 or 570-3676
Wed 11:00am-6:00pm;
Thur 1:00pm-8:00pm;
Fri-Sun 11:00am-6:00pm,
Closed Mon & Tue. Admission $6
(Free Thur 6:00pm-8:00pm)

Founded in 1930, the Whitney is considered by some the prime showcase of 20th century American art. The collection now includes the modernists (Georgia O'Keefe), cubists (Max Weber) and Abstract Expressionists such as de Kooning, Pollock, Rothko, Joan Mitchell and Helen Frankenthaler. You will also see works by Larry Poons, Robert Rauschenberg and Jasper Johns, and Pop artists Andy Warhol and Larry Rivers. The Whitney's permanent collection includes some of Paul Cadmus' homoerotic art as well. As can be expected from any attempt to assess new directions in art, the Whitney's Biennial (every odd-numbered year) generates lively controversy among art lovers in New York.

• Other New York museums of interest include:
American Craft Museum, 40 West 53rd Street (5th & 6th Avenues), ☎ 956-3535; **American Museum of the Moving Image**, 35th Avenue at 36th Street, Astoria, Queens, ☎ (718) 784-0077 (recording) and ☎ (718) 784-4777 (for travel directions), dedicated to the art, history and technology of motion pictures, TV and video; **Asia Society Gallery**, Park Avenue at 70th Street, ☎ 288-6400; **Black Fashion Museum**, 155-157 West 126th Street at Malcolm X Boulevard, ☎ 666-1320; **El Museo del Barrio**, 1230 Fifth Avenue at 104th Street, ☎ 831-7272, celebrates the Barrio, the center of Hispanic life in New York; **Fashion Institute of Technology Galleries** 227 West 27th Street at 7th Avenue, ☎ 760-7848 or 760-7760 (recording); **International Center of Photography**, 1130 Fifth Avenue at East 94th Street,

☎ 860-1777, renowned collection in a Georgian mansion, also midtown branch at 1133 6th Avenue at 43rd Street, ☎ 768-4680; **Intrepid Sea-Air Space Museum**, set in an aircraft carrier on Pier 86, West 46th Street at 12th Avenue, ☎ 245-2533 or 245-0072 (recording); **Isamu Noguchi Garden Museum**, 32-37 Vernon Boulevard at 33rd Road, Long Island City, Queens, ☎ (718) 721-1932 or (718) 204-7088 for recording which gives travel instructions and information on weekend shuttle service from Asia Society; **Jacques Marchais Center of Tibetan Art**, 338 Lighthouse Avenue, Staten Island, ☎ (718) 987-3500 or (718) 987-4378 (for recorded information), built in the style of a Buddhist monastery, houses the largest collection of Tibetan art in the West; **The Jewish Museum**, 1109 Fifth Avenue at 92nd Street, ☎ 423-3200, contains an extensive collection of Jewish artifacts and a superb collection of Marc Chagall's work; **Museum for African Art**, 593 Broadway (Prince & Houston Streets) ☎ 966-1313; **Museum of American Folk Art**, 2 Lincoln Square (63 West 60th Street/Columbus Avenue), ☎ 595-9533, 977-7298 (recording); **Museum of the City of New York**, 1220 Fifth Avenue at East 103rd Street, ☎ 534-1672; **Museum of Television and Radio**, 25 West 52nd Street (between 5th and 6th Avenues), ☎ 621-6600; **National Museum of the American Indian**, 3753 Broadway (West 155th Street), ☎ 283-2420 or 283-2497 (recording); **New Museum of Contemporary Art**, 583 Broadway (Houston & Prince Streets), ☎ 219-1222, 219-1355 (recording); **New York Transit Museum**, Schermerhorn Street and Boerum Place, Brooklyn Heights, ☎ (718) 330-3063 or (718) 330-3060 (recording), presents the history of mass transit in New York with displays of vintage subway cars; **Nicholas Roerich Museum**, 319 West 107th Street at Riverside Drive, ☎ 864-7752, exhibits the mystical art of the Nobel Peace Prize nominee who also designed sets for Diaghilev's ballets; **Police Academy Museum**, 235 East 20th Street (2nd & 3rd Avenues), ☎ 477-9753;

Socrates Sculpture Park, 31-29 Vernon Boulevard and Broadway, Long Island City, Queens, ☎ (718) 956-1819, a wild, open field with some striking work by emerging artists which is open all year round, call for directions; **The Studio Museum in Harlem**, 144 West 125th Street at Malcolm X Boulevard, ☎ 864-4500, or 865-2420 (recording); **Ukrainian Museum**, 203 Second Avenue (East 12th & 13th Streets), ☎ 228-0110.

GALLERIES

Art galleries are located principally in SoHo, on 57th Street (between 6th & Madison Avenues) and on Madison Avenue (in the 70s and 80s). Most galleries are open Tuesday through Saturday (schedules vary during the summer months). See *The New York Times, New York Magazine, Time Out New York* and the *Village Voice* for listings.

The following galleries represent gay artists and often present gay-themed or homoerotic work: **Exit Art/The First World**, 548 Broadway, ☎ 966-7745 **Feature Gallery**, 76 Greene Street (between Spring and Broome Streets), 2nd Floor, which represents the estate of Tom of Finland; **Leslie-Lohman Gay Art Foundation**, 127 Prince Street, ☎ 673-7007; **P.P.O.W**, 532 Broadway, 3rd Floor, 941-8642; and **Robert Miller Gallery**, 41 East 57th Street, ☎ 980-5454, which represents Bruce Webber and the estate of Robert Mapplethorpe.

FILM & TELEVISION

New York was a movie town before Hollywood. Some of the earliest public exhibitions of moving pictures were held in Manhattan in the late 1890s. Biograph, the studio where the great film pioneer D.W. Griffith worked, was located in New York, and so was Paramount Pictures (under the name Famous Players Company). Adolph Zukor, head of Famous Players, together with Jesse Lasky established the still functioning production facility Kaufman Astoria Studios in Queens, where the great silent stars Rudolph Valentino and Gloria Swanson once flourished.

No surprise then that New Yorkers are avid filmgoers. You'll notice long lines outside the cinemas, not only for the latest Hollywood blockbuster, but for independent and art-house movies, and of course, for any opening of a new film by New York's celebrated auteurs — Woody Allen, Martin Scorsese and Spike Lee.

Check out the giant Sony IMAX 3-D cinema at the Sony Lincoln Square complex at West 68th Street and Broadway. A particular favorite with visitors to New York is *Across the Sea of Time*, a 50-minute which shows-off the city in 3D splendor, incorporating stunning stereoptic photographs of turn-of-the-century New York.

For information on first-run movies playing at cinemas near you ☎ 777-FILM (777-3456). Bear in mind that tickets are sold out hours in advance for very popular films, especially in the first week of their release, and the queue you see may be for ticket *holders* and not for buyers. You can also charge tickets in advance on your credit card in many cinemas.

The New York Film Festival, held at the Lincoln Center in September, presents the cream of the international festivals — Cannes, Venice and Berlin — and new American features and shorts. More avant-garde works and promising first films are showcased at **New Directors/New Films**, presented in March at the Museum of Modern Art.

GAY & LESBIAN FILM

Gay-themed films occasionally get commercial releases at New York art-house cinemas, but the best opportunity to view the diverse range of current gay and lesbian filmmaking is during the city's two annual gay film and video events:

THE NEW YORK LESBIAN & GAY FILM FESTIVAL

47 Great Jones Street, 6th Floor
New York, NY 10012
☎ 254-7228 Fax: 254-8655

Usually held in June, the Festival is, along with the San Francisco and Los Angeles festivals, one of the prime venues for showcasing the work of American and international gay filmmakers in the U.S.

NEW YORK LESBIAN AND GAY EXPERIMENTAL FILM/VIDEO FESTIVAL

c/o Jim Hubbard, 503 Broadway
Room 503, New York, NY 10012
☎ 925 5883

Held in the 2nd and 3rd weeks of September — this is the only gay festival devoted entirely to experimental work.

TELEVISION

All the daily newspapers, as well as *Time Out New York* carry television viewing guides. The major networks broadcast on the following channels: Channel 2 — CBS; Channel 4 — NBC; Channel 7 — ABC and Channel 5 — Fox Television. The city's public television station, Channel 13, provides cultural and educational programming, British programs and, in the month of June, gay- related programming. If you find yourself "channel surfing" on late-night cable TV in Manhattan, check out the public access channels for some of the tackiest and the most outrageous programs in the country.

GAY TELEVISION

Gay TV programs and semi-porn entertainment are carried on the public access cable channels. The most popular shows are GAY USA and MEN AND FILMS presented by the Gay Cable Network, and THE HEDDA LETTUCE SHOW. Check out the ROBIN BYRD SHOW and her "Men on Men" programs which feature male strippers and porn celebrities (not available in some areas in Manhattan). *HX* and *Next's* television guides will keep you up to date on programs of gay interest.

GAY CABLE NETWORK

150 West 26th Street, Suite 703
New York, NY 10001
☎ 727-8850

Founded in 1982, GCN produces weekly news, information and entertainment programming for gays and lesbians and now reaches over 30 markets.

IN THE LIFE

39 West 14th Street, Suite 402
New York, NY 10013
☎ 255-6012

A gay and lesbian variety series presented on many public television stations throughout the U.S.

LAVENDER SOUL PRODUCTIONS (video collective)

☎ 749-0405; Attn: Nancy Kitron

Produces *The Pulse*, a cable show for and by People of Color, Lesbian, Gay, Bisexual & TwoSpirit.

GAY NEW YORK IN LITERATURE, THEATER AND FILM

BOOKS:

And the Band Played On, Randy Shilts; *Another Country*, James Baldwin; *The Beauty of Men*, Andrew Holleran; *City Poet, biography of Frank O Hara*, Brad Gooch; *Capote: A Biography*, Gerald Clarke; *City of Night*, John Rechy; *Dancer from the Dance*, Andrew Holleran; *Empathy*, Sarah Schulman; *Faggots*, Larry Kramer; *The Family of Max Desir*, Robert Ferro; *The Front Runner*, Patricia Nell Warren; *Hold Tight*, Christopher Bram; *The Irreversible Decline of Eddy Socket*, John Weir; *Latin Moon in Manhattan*, Jamie Manrique; *The Lost Language of Cranes*, David Leavitt; *A Low Life in High Heels*, Holly Woodlawn; *The Lure*, Felice Picano; *Memoirs of a Bastard Angel*, Harold Norse; *Scared Lips of the Bronx*, Douglas Sadowick; *States of Desire*, Edmund White; *Stonewall*, Martin Duberman; *Temple Slave*, Robert Patrick.

PLAYS:

Angels in America, Tony Kushner; *As Is*, William Hoffman; *The Boys in the Band*, Mart Crowley; *A Chorus Line*, James Kirkwood, Marvin Hamlisch; *The Destiny of Me*, Larry Kramer; *Falsettos*, William Finn; *The Haunted Host*, Robert Patrick; *Jeffrey*, Paul Rudnick; *Love! Valour! Compassion!*, Terrence McNally; *The Night Larry Kramer Kissed Me*, David Drake; *The Normal Heart*, Larry Kramer; *The Ritz*, Terrence McNally; *Street Theater*, Doric Wilson; *Torch Song Trilogy*, Harvey Fierstein.

MOVIES:

Before Stonewall; The Boys in the Band; Cruising (warning: homophobic!); *Jeffrey; Longtime Companion; Midnight Cowboy; Parting Glances; Paris is Burning; The Ritz; Stonewall; Torch Song Trilogy; Wigstock:The Movie.*

See Chapter 11 for information on bookstores, and places to rent/buy videotapes. Non-U.S. visitors: note the American video system is incompatible with video systems in use elsewhere in the world.

11: SHOPPING

by Jeff Stockwell

They come from São Paulo and Brussels, Tokyo and Karachi. And they come for one reason: to SHOP! Almost any type of goods can be bought in New York, and often at an excellent price. Clothing, electronics, jewelry, books, and records of the best quality and widest variety are all to be found in the Big Apple.

The gay shopping experience begins on **Christopher Street** in **Greenwich Village**. Between 6th Avenue and Hudson Street you will find jewelry, leather, and men's clothing stores, as well as erotic card, novelty, and video shops.

If you find yourself visiting the **Upper West Side** while in New York, there are a number of wonderful gift shops, clothing boutiques, and bookstores on **Columbus** and **Amsterdam** avenues between the low 70s and the high 80s. **Aventura** has a particularly stunning collection of modern Venetian glass.

SoHo should be avoided on the weekends. The streets there are so overrun with tourists (no offense) on Saturday and Sunday afternoons that you can barely navigate the sidewalks. On quieter weekdays, however, you can visit some of the city's most exciting contemporary art galleries or shop at **Putumayo,** which sells beautiful Mexican and South American clothes, fabrics, and handcrafts.

Fifth Avenue, between 48th and 59th Streets, has some of the most elegant and exclusive stores in the world: **Tiffany & Co., Harry Winston, Bulgari, Takashimaya, Cartier, Fendi, Saks Fifth Avenue, Bergdorf Goodman** and **Gucci** all line this stretch. In addition, many of the city's most prestigious art galleries are located around 5th Avenue and 57th Street.

The **Upper East Side, Madison** and **Lexington** avenues, between 59th and 96th Streets, are dotted with elegant little boutiques. China, crystal, and silver shops are found interspersed with the fine art and antique galleries that line Madison Avenue. **Barney's** uptown and **Calvin Klein** are two of the newer and larger additions to Madison Avenue.

If you are looking for high quality diamonds and/or gold, and prefer a much lower pricetag than you will find at Tiffany (although you must visit Tiffany), then investigate the **Diamond District**, 47th Street between 5th and 6th Avenues. **Gold Emporium Inc.** is gay-friendly and gives a portion of its profits to the Gay Men's Health Crisis Center.

For terrific discounts on leather jackets, briefcases, luggage and shoes, as well as fabrics and small electronics, visit Orchard Street on the **Lower East Side**. Because most establishments in this neighborhood are owned by Orthodox Jews, the great majority of Lower East Side shops close early on Friday and do not open on Saturday. These shops are, however, open on Sunday.

The businesses listed below sell items that many tourists want to buy while in New York. If you are looking for something that is not listed in this book, consult the Manhattan Yellow Pages. Unless noted otherwise, all phone numbers listed in this chapter are in the 212 area code.

Store hours vary widely, so if you are planning to visit a particular establishment, it is best to call first. Also, remember that an 8.25% sales tax is added to almost all purchases made in New York City.

AUCTIONS

CHRISTIE'S

520 Park Avenue/ 58th Street
☎ 546-1000; 371-5438 (24 hour recorded information)
If you're looking to add to your collections of Judy Garland memorabilia, 18th-century American tilt-top tea tables, or Spanish Baroque paintings, Christie's auction house is worth a visit. Most of the previews and the auctions are open to the general public.

CHRISTIE'S EAST

219 East 67th Street/ 2nd & 3rd Avenues
☎ 606-0400; 371-5438 (24 hour recorded information)
Christie's East auctions lower-market items than its Park Avenue parent.

SOTHEBY'S

1334 York Avenue/ 72nd Street
☎ 606-7000
The American-owned rival of Christie's auctions an amazing variety of items: wines, coins, sporting equipment, paintings, drawings, prints, sculpture, silver, porcelain, etcetera.

WILLIAM DOYLE

175 East 87th Street/ Lexington & 3rd Avenues

☎ 427-2730

William Doyle specializes in English and American furniture and decorative arts, and places less of an emphasis than Christie's and Sotheby's on fine art.

ANTIQUES

• There are three areas of Manhattan with large concentrations of antique dealers. Along 57th Street, between 3rd and 6th Avenues, there are a number of very fine and very expensive stores. On Broadway, between 9th and 20th Streets, and on University Place, between 9th and 12th Streets, there are also many elegant antique shops, some of which are open only to decorators and dealers: the trade. The third area is upper Madison and Lexington Avenues, between 79th and 96th Streets.

If you like flea-markets, the following two are particularly good for silver, clothing, knick-knacks, and cute men a-shopping.

ANNEX ANTIQUES FAIR & FLEA MARKET

6th Avenue from 24th-26th Streets

☎ 243-5343

Sat & Sun 9:00am-5:00pm

Although the official starting time is 9:00 am, one can arrive as early as 5:00 am when most of the booths open and most of the best merchandise sells fast.

J.S. FLEA MARKET

Columbus Avenue/ 77th & 78th Streets

☎ 316-1088

Sun, 10:00am-8:30pm

BLUE JEANS & CASUALS

CANAL JEAN COMPANY

504 Broadway/ Broome & Spring Streets

☎ 226-1130

Canal Jean Company sells all styles and sizes of Levis, t-shirts, jeans, sportswear, and accessories in its 50,000 square foot SoHo store. Many good bargains can be found here.

CHELSEA ARMY AND NAVY

110 8th Avenue/ 15th & 16th Streets

☎ 645-7420

59TH STREET ARMY AND NAVY

221 East 59th Street/ 2nd & 3rd Avenues

☎ 755-1855

DAVE'S ARMY AND NAVY

799 Sixth Avenue/ 26th Street
☎ 989-6444

2ND AVENUE ARMY AND NAVY

1598 2nd Avenue/ 83rd Street
☎ 737-4661

VILLAGE ARMY AND NAVY

328 Bleecker Street/ Christopher Street
☎ 242-6665

Each of these Army and Navy stores sells every existing size and color of Levi's, including the popular 501, 505, 550, 560, and Silver Tab jeans. They also sell bomber jackets, fatigue pants, bandannas, and an assortment of military insignia and badges.

BOOKSTORES

BARNES AND NOBLE SUPERSTORES

105 5th Avenue/ 18th Street
☎ 807-0099
2289 Broadway/ 82nd Street
☎ 362-8835
4 Astor Place/ Lafayette
☎ 420-1322
675 6th Avenue/ 22nd Street
☎ 727-1227
600 5th Avenue/ 48th Street
☎ 765-0590
Citicorp Building/ Madison and 54th Streets
☎ 362-8835
1280 Lexington Avenue/ 86th Street
☎ 423-9900
1972 Broadway/ 66th Street
☎ 595-6859

The Barnes and Noble at 18th Street and 5th Avenue advertises itself as the world's largest bookstore, and it may well be. Across the street, on the west side of 5th Avenue, is a sale annex, where enormous discounts are offered on a wide range of titles. The new superstores, which seem to be taking over city blocks at an alarming rate, feature Starbucks espresso bars, comfortable chairs for reading, and around a quarter of a million books per location. The gay and lesbian section at the Broadway and 82nd Street store is said to be a good place to meet fellow bibliophiles.

RIZZOLI

31 West 57th Street/ 5th & 6th Avenues
☎ 759-2424
454 West Broadway, in SoHo
☎ 674-1616
200 Vesey Street, in the World Financial Center
☎ 385-1400

Every bit as exceptional as the art books produced by Rizzoli Publishing, these bookstores sell a full range of art, architecture, music, fiction, and history titles, as well as classical and jazz compact disks and tapes.

THE STRAND

828 Broadway/ 12th Street
☎ 473-1452
159 John Street/ South Street Seaport
☎ 809-0875

Tucked away on the shelves are books once owned and/or written by some of Manhattan's most famous inhabitants. You're bound to find something of interest among the tens of thousands of second-hand books scattered throughout the Strand. However don't expect much cooperation from their sometimes less-than-helpful staff.

THREE LIVES

154 West 10th Street/ Waverly Place
☎ 741-2069

An intimate corner bookshop, with gay friendly environment, carrying a good general selection of titles.

GAY BOOKSTORES

A DIFFERENT LIGHT

151 West 19th Street/ 6th & 7th Avenues
☎ 989-4850

A Different Light offers a selection of over 15,000 gay and lesbian books and an extensive assortment of homoerotic magazines. The store also sponsors many poetry and prose readings and has a coffee bar.

CREATIVE VISIONS BOOKS

548 Hudson Street, (between Charles & Perry Streets)
☎ 645-7573

Promoted as being as charming and inviting as Greenwich Village itself, this gay and lesbian bookstore has a wide range of lesbian, gay, bisexual, transgender and women's interest books and a friendly coffee bar. It's the highbrow sister to Gay Pleasures, which is located next-door and specializes in erotic fare.

OSCAR WILDE MEMORIAL BOOKSHOP

15 Christopher Street/ 6th & 7th Avenues
☎ 255-8097

Founded in 1967, Oscar Wilde is New York City's oldest exclusively gay and lesbian bookstore.

DEPARTMENT & MEN'S SPECIALTY STORES

BARNEY S

Madison Avenue/ 61st Street
☎ 826-8900
7th Avenue/ 17th Street
☎ 929-9000
2 World Financial Center, at 225 Liberty Street
☎ 945-1600

Once Barney's downsized its 7th Avenue venue and opened the new flagship store on Madison Avenue common knowledge became indisputable fact: the store that began by selling discounted mens clothing in the once-unfashionable Chelsea has transformed itself into one of the most elegant and sophisticated shopping experiences known to humankind. Barney's sells the latest and best in men's fashions and accessories (as well as women's fashions and housewares). Styles run the gamut, from conservative English and American suits to the newest styles from Paris and Milan. Make sure to take note of the innovative window displays. The 7th Avenue store is very gay. Unfortunately, the sales help can sometimes feel themselves above assisting mere customers, but they are usually courteous enough with queens.

BLOOMINGDALE'S

Lexington Avenue/ 59th Street
☎ 705-2000

Bloomingdale's, like Barney s, began as a discount store. As it grew, its simpler forms were masked by thin layers of black marble and shiny brass. Escalators, elevators, and staircases go every which way, and never seem to get you to your destination on the first try. And don't even think of asking a salesperson for help. All of this being said, Bloomingdale's sells fine things at moderate to expensive prices. Gay men have been known to make new friends while shopping here.

BERGDORF GOODMAN FOR MEN

5th Avenue/ 58th Street

☎ 753-7300

The latest and the best in international fashion are available here at extremely high prices. Oxford shirts can easily run $150.00 each at what is arguably the most glamorous store in Manhattan.

BROOKS BROTHERS

346 Madison Avenue/ 44th Street

☎ 682-8800

Since 1818, Brooks Brothers has offered the best selection and quality in conservative clothing for men. Although the name is world famous, the prices are quite reasonable.

CENTURY 21

22 Cortland Street

☎ 227-9092

Designer brands are sold here at fantastically discounted prices. There aren't any fitting rooms, but they will let you return items. Save your receipts!

LORD & TAYLOR

5th Avenue/ 38th Street

☎ 391-3344

This beautiful department store takes one back to New York as it was glamorized in the first half of this century. Lord & Taylor specializes in American designers.

MACY'S

34th Street/ Broadway

☎ 695-4400

Macy's is simply the largest department store in the world. Almost anything and everything is sold here, and everyone seems to be buying it at the same time. Even if you don't plan on buying anything, a visit to Macy's is well worth the sight.

MOE GINSBURG

162 5th Avenue/ 21st & 22nd Streets

☎ 242-3482

An excellent selection of European and American suits, shoes, formalwear, and sportswear is available here at discounted prices.

SAKS FIFTH AVENUE

5th Avenue/ 49th Street

☎ 753-4000

Saks sells high-quality clothing and accessories at high prices. The calm and gracious environment of this elegantly-appointed store sets it in a different world from the hustle-bustle-razzmatazz of Macy's and Bloomingdale s.

ELECTRONICS

BI-RIGHT PHOTO & ELECTRONICS

15 East 30th Street/ 5th & Madison Avenues
☎ 685-2130
You should know what you want before you go in, but the prices are extremely attractive.

J&R MUSIC WORLD

23 Park Row, just south of City Hall
☎ 732-8600
Televisions, video-cassette recorders, computer and stereo equipment as well as compact disks, video games and video cassettes are all sold at discount prices at this reputable downtown institution.

THE WIZ

726 4th Street/ Broadway;
6th Avenue/ 8th Street;
17 Union Square West/ 15th Street;
31st Street/ 6th Avenue;
33rd Street/ 5th Avenue;
48 West 45th Street/ 5th & 6th Avenues;
212 East 57th Street/ 2nd & 3rd Avenues;
86th Street/ 3rd Avenue;
97th Street/ Broadway
For information and store hours call
☎ 908-602-1950
Nobody beats the Wiz, so the advertisement reads, and they claim that they will beat any price in town. To get them to honor this promise, however, you may have to do some haggling. They sell a full line of electronic, audio, and video goods.

EROTICA

CONDOMANIA

351 Bleecker Street/ West 10th Street
☎ 691-9442
Condomania sells condoms in an enticing variety of shapes, sizes, and colors. They also sell gifts, both practical and playful.

DAVID SAMUEL MENKES CUSTOM LEATHER WEAR

144 5th Avenue/ 19th Street. 3rd floor (by appointment)
☎ 989-3706
For the ultimate in heavy duty leather and bondage goods, and a wild assortment of toys, give David Menkes a call. He makes everything to order, so let your imagination run riot.

THE GAUNTLET

144 5th Avenue/ 19th Street. 2nd floor
☎ 229-0180
If you care to have your ears or any other body parts pierced, and can prove that you are over 18 years old, this is the place to go.

GAY PLEASURES

546 Hudson Street/ Charles & Perry Streets
☎ 255-5756
A tremendously wide range of erotica, including vintage gay porn, can be purchased at this Village institution.

THE LEATHERMAN

111 Christopher Street
☎ 243-5339
The Leatherman features a full selection of leather and latex jackets, pants, chaps, vests, boots, etc, as well as a specialty dungeon in which you will find videos, magazines, and other assorted goodies.

NEW YORK CITY CUSTOM LEATHER

312 East 9th Street/ 1st & 2nd Avenues
☎ 674-3895
Everything is custom made at this top-quality, top-price leather store. Made-to-fit pants start at $600 a pair.

THE NOOSE

261 West 19th Street/ 7th & 8th Avenues
☎ 807-1789
For the latest in leather, latex, and bondage equipment, visit The Noose.

THE PLEASURE CHEST

156 7th Avenue South/ Perry & Charles Streets
☎ 242-4185
The name says it all; be sure to check out the erotic cards.

FUN & GAMES

F.A.O. SCHWARZ

767 5th Avenue/ 58th Street
☎ 644-9400
Even if you don't plan on buying any toys, F.A.O. Schwarz is worth a visit. Spending half an hour in this sophisticated fantasyland is a wonderful respite from a day of serious shopping on Fifth Avenue.

HAMMACHER SCHLEMMER

147 East 57th Street/ Lexington & 3rd Avenues
☎ 421-9000
Hammacher Schlemmer provides one with the little things, like electric socks and personalized hovercrafts, that make life just a bit easier.

THE GAME SHOW

474 5th Avenue
☎ 633-6328
1240 Lexington Avenue/ 83rd & 84th Streets
☎ 472-8011
The Game Show stocks hundreds upon hundreds of games, puzzles, toys and reference books for both children and adults. They also sell collectible games and toys.

THE SHARPER IMAGE

89 South Street Seaport/ Pier 17
☎ 693-0477
4 West 57th Street
☎ 265-2550
The Sharper Image doesn't sell anything that a human being truly needs, but some of their high-tech gadgets are a great deal of fun.

MUSIC & VIDEO

HMV

2081 Broadway/ 72nd Street
☎ 721-5900
1280 Lexington Avenue/ 86th Street
☎ 348-0800
HMV offers a wide range of classical, opera, rock, jazz, blues, folk and show music.

KIM'S MUSIC AND VIDEO

144 Bleecker Street/ LaGuardia Place
☎ 260-1010
350 Bleecker Street/ West 10th Street
☎ 675-8996
6th St. Mark's Place (site of St. Mark's bath house)
☎ 598-9985
133 2nd Avenue/ St. Mark's Place
☎ 505-0311
85 Avenue A/ 5th & 6th Streets
☎ 529-3410
Kim's provides a good selection of art-house movies, gay and lesbian documentaries and feature films, and male pornography.

TOWER RECORDS AND VIDEO

692 Broadway/ East 4th Street
☎ 505-1500
2107 Broadway/ 73rd-74th Streets
☎ 799-2500
Tower carries one of the most comprehensive selections of compact disks and cassette tapes in Manhattan. The Village location has adjacent video and book stores. The West Side location, which is temporary while a new skyscraper rises above its old/soon-to-be-new home at 1961 Broadway, has a large video section upstairs.

VIRGIN MEGASTORE

1540 Broadway/ 45th-46th Streets
☎ 921-1020
Recently opened in Times Square, Virgin claims their three-level, 75,000 square foot Manhattan flagship is the world's largest purveyor of music, movies, books and multimedia products.

SHOW BUSINESS BOOKS & RECORDINGS

APPLAUSE THEATRE BOOKS

211 West 71st Street/ Broadway
☎ 496-7511
Visit Applause for the best selection of books on theater and film, and a vast collection of playscripts and screenplays.

THE DRAMA BOOK SHOP

723 7th Avenue/ 48th Street. 2nd floor

☎ 944-0595

The Drama bookshop houses thousands of books on film, television, dance, and theater, as well as play, film, and television scripts.

FOOTLIGHT RECORDS

113 East 12th Street

☎ 533-1572

For Garland, Merman, and Streisand recordings, this is the place to shop. Footlight claims to have the largest selection available anywhere of Broadway and foreign cast albums and film sound tracks. They also sell operetta, big band, jazz, and rock recordings.

SHOW BUSINESS MEMORABILIA

ACTORS HERITAGE

262 West 44th Street/ 8th Avenue & Broadway

☎ 944-9490

Located next door to the St.James theater, this store is a good place to find Broadway musical souvenir books, t-shirts, cast albums and theater books, and postcards.

MOVIE STAR NEWS

134 West 18th Street/ 6th & 7th Avenues

☎ 620-8160

Every type of movie star photo, scene still, and film poster can be found at this Chelsea store. A great array of press books and other publicity materials are also sold here.

ONE SCHUBERT ALLEY

One Schubert Alley, connecting 44th and 45th Streets/ Broadway & 8th Avenue

☎ 586-7610

Broadway posters, t-shirts, recordings, and books are all sold here.

12: EATING OUT

by Jeff Stockwell

With residents of almost every nationality in New York, it is possible to sample virtually any type of cuisine in the city. You can begin the day with an American-style breakfast, enjoy lunch at a Village bistro, have tea at one of Manhattan's great hotels, and dine at one of the city's many African, Arabic, Cuban, Thai, Ukrainian, or West Indian restaurants.

Since it is impossible to provide in one chapter a comprehensive survey of Manhattan's restaurants, I have chosen to list some of my personal favorites. For a more complete listing of generally popular restaurants, consult *The New Yorker* or *New York Magazine*. To locate gay and gay-friendly restaurants other than the ones listed below, consult the *HX* , *Next* and *The Native*.

If you find yourself looking for a restaurant as you wander through a neighborhood, here are some general guidelines. First, check the front windows for restaurant reviews. You may find that some of the posted reviews are ten years old, but if the restaurant ever served a decent meal, someone will have taken note. Second, try to avoid restaurants near tourist sites. While there are many good finds within ten minutes of Times Square, the Empire State Building, and Museum Mile, you may have to search for them. It is worth an extra few minutes of walking to avoid a Houlihans or Howard Johnson's. Restaurants on Sixth and Seventh Avenues in Midtown, from the low 40s through the high 50s, are particularly well-known for mediocre food and high prices. It is in reference to such establishments that tourists return home complaining of $12.00 hamburgers. Instead of wasting your money at a midtown tourist trap, walk over to **9th Avenue,** between 43rd and 57th Streets, where you will find a number of good and inexpensive bistros, pizza joints, and Greek diners. (Most of the diners in New York are run by Greek families. It's best to order either traditional Greek or American fare at these restaurants. Never order Mexican food at a Greco-American diner!)

The **East Village**, especially the area around Avenue A from 4th to 14th Streets, houses some of the best and cheapest restaurants and coffee houses in Manhattan. They also provide a space from which to watch bohemians, beggars, and businesspeople go about their lives in relative harmony, living both very much together and very much apart. If you care for Indian food, there are many inexpensive restaurants on **Curry Row**, Sixth Street between First and Second Avenues. The food at most of these restaurants is of a similar quality; you will pay a little more for leg room, attentive service, and pleasant surroundings.

Finally, don't be wary of food sold from street vendors; it's usually fresh and of high quality. Hot dogs and sausages, falafel, souvlaki, and gyros are everyday fare for many New Yorkers. If you happen to wander up Sixth Avenue in the 50s around lunch time, you will see thousands of office workers munching on food purchased at these carts. All of the restaurants listed below are in the 212 area code, unless otherwise noted. Reservations at the finest restaurants must often be made three to four weeks in advance. If you simply must dine at Bouley or Cafe Des Artistes, however, and have only a few days before you leave New York, call and see if they have any last minute cancellations.

AMERICAN

CLAIRE

156 7th Avenue/ 19th & 20th Streets
☎ 255-1955
This seafood restaurant was gay before Chelsea was. Good, fresh foods at reasonable prices. The key-lime pie is a specialty.

CIRCA

103 2nd Avenue/ East 6th Street
☎ 777-4120
Fags are everywhere in this East Village restaurant that specializes in New American Cuisine. Dress to impress — a simple strand of pearls is always nice with your biker jacket.

DAVID'S POT BELLY RESTAURANT

94 Christopher Street/ Bleecker Street
☎ 242-8036
A gay landmark that serves tasty, inexpensive fare late into the night. If the weather is clement, ask to dine in the garden.

EIGHTEEN & EIGHTH

159 8th Avenue/ 18th Street
☎ 242-5000
Long lines form here for trendy updates of traditional American cuisine. The waiters are often as delectable as the cuisine. A Chelsea must.

ELEPHANT AND CASTLE

68 Greenwich Avenue/ 7th Avenue
☎ 243-1400
Good, casual food. Gay friendly. Very popular (and crowded) for weekend brunches and dinners.

EMPIRE DINER

210 10th Avenue/ 22nd Street
☎ 243-2736
This upscale diner, which is open 24 hours a day, becomes gayer and gayer as the night goes on. A mixed restaurant at six in the evening, The Empire is a last stop for drag divas before calling it a night.

FLAMINGO EAST

219 2nd Avenue/ 13th Street
☎ 533-2860
They serve good food to great-looking men at this East Village restaurant. The atmosphere here is a little off-beat and a lot of fun.

MUSEUM CAFE

366 Columbus Avenue/ 77th Street
☎ 799-0150
This restaurant is a wonderful respite after a day of shopping on Columbus Avenue or touring the Museum of Natural History, which is just across the street. The salads here are excellent.

PISCES
95 Avenue A/ 6th Street
☎ 260-6660
Some of the best fish in New York is served at this trendy and always-busy East Village restaurant. Moderately priced.

POPOVER CAFE
551 Amsterdam Avenue/ 86th & 87th Streets
☎ 595-8555
The popovers here are hot, soft, and always fresh. This is an especially nice place for lunch or weekend brunch.

ROYAL CANADIAN PANCAKE HOUSE
2286 Broadway/ West 82nd Street
☎ 873-6052
1004 2nd Avenue/ East 53rd Street
☎ 980-4131
The portions served here are obscene, but the food is top quality and the prices low.

UNION SQUARE CAFE
21 East 16th Street/ 5th & 6th Avenues
☎ 243-4020
With its innovative cuisine and fashionable customers, the Union Square Cafe is considered by many to be one of the best restaurants in Manhattan. Entrees cost between $15.00 and $25.00. If you happen to be in the neighborhood on a Wednesday or Saturday, stroll through the Greenmarket held across the street in Union Square. The Amish baked goods sold there are particularly good.

UNIVERSAL GRILL
44 Bedford Street/ 6th & 7th Avenues
☎ 989-5621
With a gay environment, good food, and reasonable prices, this Village restaurant is comfortable for breakfast, lunch, dinner, or weekend brunch.

BAGELS and SUCH

ESS-A-BAGEL
359 1st Avenue/ 20th & 21st Streets
☎ 260-2252
Many Manhattanites consider the bagels at Ess-A-Bagel to be the best in New York City (which means the best bagels in the world).

H & H BAGELS
2239 Broadway/ 80th Street
☎ 595-8003
1551 2nd Avenue
☎ 734-7441
Once you've eaten an H & H bagel, you'll understand why they sell over 10,000 of them each day.

ZABAR'S

2245 Broadway/ 81st Street
☎ 787-2000

Although Zabar's isn't a restaurant, it's a culinary treat that can't be missed. Here you will find the best chocolates, smoked salmon, strudel, cheese, and coffee in Manhattan at a fraction of the costs other establishments charge. At Zabar's Food-To-Go, you can buy what is perhaps the best breakfast deal in town: a piping hot cup of Zabar's coffee, a glass of freshly squeezed orange juice, and a croissant stuffed with egg, cheese, and ham, all for $3.00.

CELEBRITY HAUNTS

ORSO RESTAURANT

322 West 46th Street/ 8th & 9th Avenues
☎ 489-7212

Restaurant Row is a block of restaurants on West 46th Street that caters to the pre-and-post theater crowds. Most of the establishments are in the middle price range, with entrees running from $12.00 to $25.00. While these restaurants are close to many theaters, the food is often merely adequate. Orso's is an exception. The food here is excellent, reasonably priced Italian fare, and you are quite likely to see Lauren Bacall or Roddy McDowall dining a few tables away from you. Reservations are advised.

SARDIS

234 West 44th Street/ 7th & 8th Avenues
☎ 221-8440

As the food here is mediocre and expensive, try Sardis for dessert or an after-dinner drink that will give you enough time to see any celebrities and to take in the thousands of caricatures of show business personalities that fill every available inch of wall space. Reservations advised.

CHINESE

• It is hard to walk more than two or three blocks in Manhattan without passing a Chinese restaurant. Most of them serve decent, albeit often oily, food. The restaurants listed below are particularly good, and except at Dish of Salt, the meals rarely cost more than $15.00 a person, including tax and tip.

CHARLIE MOM

47 7th Avenue South, Greenwich Village
☎ 255-2848
464 6th Ave/ 11th Street
☎ 807-8585

An entree at Charlie Mom may cost a few dollars more than one at the run-of-the-mill neighborhood Chinese restaurant, but it's well worth it. For $10.00 to $15.00 you can enjoy an excellent meal.

DISH OF SALT

133 West 47th Street/ 6th & 7th Avenues

☎ 921-4242

Excellent Cantonese cuisine served in a spacious, stylish, quiet setting. Moderate to high prices. Perhaps the most elegant Chinese meal to be found in New York City. Reservations advised.

GOLDEN UNICORN

18 East Broadway

☎ 941-0911

Those who consider themselves knowledgeable about Chinese cuisine usually pick the Golden Unicorn over all other Chinatown restaurants. Prospective diners often have trouble finding the Golden Unicorn, but once they do they are almost never disappointed.

GREAT SHANG HAI RESTAURANT

47 Division Street

☎ 966-7663

Dumplings are a specialty at this Chinatown venue which serves authentic Shanghai cuisine.

20 MOTT STREET

20 Mott Street

☎ 964-0380

This Chinatown restaurant serves excellent dim sum (literally translated as little bits of heart) upstairs, and full meals in the basement. After your meal, buy a cone of Chinese ice cream as you wander through Chinatown; Green Tea and Almond Cookie are particularly good flavors.

COFFEE BARS

CAFE LA FORTUNA

69 West 71st Street/ Central Park West & Columbus Avenue

☎ 724-5846.

John Lennon and Yoko Ono used to hang out at the Upper West Side staple. Great Tiramisu.

BIG CUP TEA & COFFEE

228 8th Avenue/ 21st & 22nd Streets

☎ 206-0059

The name says it all. Perhaps the most popular hangout in gay Chelsea; a comfy place to make new friends or relax with old ones. Monday is bingo night.

CHELSEA'S

210 7th Avenue

☎ 206-8033

Delicious pastries.

THE HUNGARIAN PASTRY SHOP

1030 Amsterdam Avenue/ 111th & 112th Streets
☎ 866-4230

You may be surprised to find that this pastry shop is more Euro-bohemian than anything you've encountered on the Continent. People sit here for hours reading Proust, writing their dissertations, or just watching the crowds. Good pastries and coffee. This place is a nice respite if you've just toured the Cathedral of St. John the Divine or if you're looking to meet a Columbia undergraduate.

CONTINENTAL

THE CENTURY CAFE

132 West 43rd Street/ 6th Avenue & Broadway
☎ 398-1988

Serving excellent food in an architecturally interesting environment, The Century Cafe is one of the best finds in the mid-town area. Most entrees are between $15 00 and $20.00. This restaurant is perfect for a pre-theater dinner.

CORNELIA STREET CAFE

29 Cornelia Street/ Bleecker & West 4th Streets
☎ 989-9319

A lovely and inexpensive little cafe, quietly tucked away in the Village. The breakfasts and lunches are quite inexpensive, and more satisfying than the dinners.

TOWNHOUSE RESTAURANT

206 East 58th Street/ 2nd & 3rd Avenues
☎ 826-6241

The Townhouse is the gayest restaurant on the Upper East Side. The prix fixe dinner is around $15.00. After dinner, it's just a short stroll down the block to the Townhouse Bar.

TRIBECA GRILL

375 Greenwich Street/ Franklin Street
☎ 941-3900

Robert DiNiro, Bill Murray, Christopher Walken, Mikhail Baryshnikov, Lou Diamond Phillips, Ed Harris, and Sean Penn are co-owners of this elegant restaurant. Dress well to see and be seen (the waiters here are uniformly attractive) at this expensive and popular venue. Reservations are imperative.

DELICATESSENS

• Carnegie and Wolf's are but two of several delicatessens in the West 50s. The sandwiches are expensive, around $8.00 to $10.00 a piece, but they are also enormous (weighing up to 2lbs.), and can easily be shared by two people. Carnegie is probably more famous, but I prefer Wolf's as the atmosphere there is less frenetic. New York Delicatessen, which is located at 57th Street between 6th and 7th Avenues, should be avoided; the food quality is poor and the prices are high.

CARNEGIE DELICATESSEN

854 7th Avenue/ 55th Street

☎ 757-2245

Open from 6:30am-3:30am seven days a week, this New York City institution specializes in oversized sandwiches (the pastrami and corned beef are particularly popular) and blintzes.

WOLF'S RESTAURANT AND DELI

101 West 57th Street/ 6th Avenue

☎ 586-1110

Moderately priced, huge sandwiches. Perfect if you need a quick meal before a performance at Carnegie Hall, or want a simple cup of coffee and piece of New York cheesecake after.

ENGLISH TEA

Afternoon tea is served at most of the great New York hotels (The Carlyle, The Plaza, The Pierre, The Stanhope, etc.), as well as at several Greenwich Village tea shops. Those listed below are my personal favorites.

ANGLERS AND WRITERS

420 Hudson Street at St. Luke's Place, just south of Christopher Street

☎ 675-0810

This Village tea shop is wonderfully eclectic.

CIII RESTAURANT

103 Waverly Place, at the Washington Square Hotel

☎ 254-1200

This cozy little basement restaurant at the north-west corner of Washington Square Park is one of the Village's hidden jewels. They serve lunch, tea, and dinner, but before evening you can often have the restaurant to yourself. The tea menu, which consists of sandwiches, scones, and desserts, as well as a pot of tea for each person, is excellent.

THE PEMBROKE ROOM

at the Lowell Hotel

28 East 63rd Street, east of 5th Avenue

☎ 838-1400

This elegant and reserved restaurant is located in what many consider the finest hotel in New York. The Pembroke Room forgoes the flash so often associated with New York, serving instead refined cuisine in a delightfully peaceful setting.

TEA & SYMPATHY

108 Greenwich Avenue/ 7th Avenue & Hudson Street
☎ 807-8329

Years from now, when you think of this little Village tea shop (and you will), your thoughts will be more than kind.

FRENCH

BOULEY

165 Duane Street/ Greenwich & Hudson Streets
☎ 608-3852

Although dinner at this sumptuous TriBeCa restaurant will easily cost you $100.00 per person, it may also be the most gratifying culinary experience of your life. The prix fixe tasting lunch, $32.00, and the prix fixe tasting dinner, $70.00, are highly recommended. Jackets and ties are required. Reservations are imperative, and often must be made many weeks in advance.

CAFE DES ARTISTES

1 West 67th Street, just off Central Park West
☎ 877-3500

Expensive, elegant, and a perfect thank you gift for the West Side friends who've put you up for a week in their apartment, Cafe des Artistes is one of my favorite restaurants. Reservations must often be made a week or two in advance, and jackets and ties are required. Cafe des Artistes serves both early and late meals to accommodate the pre-and-post theater crowds.

DANIEL

20 East 76th Street/ 5th & Madison Avenues
☎ 288-0033

Excellent French cuisine. Don't forget: jackets, ties, and reservations

FLORENT RESTAURANT

69 Gansevoort Street, near Greenwich Street
☎ 989-5779

Many people love the ambiance o this tres trendy French food dine in Manhattan's meat-packing dis trict (yes, that was a doubl entendre). I personally don't lik trekking fifteen minutes from th train for expensive diner fare. Th after-hours crowd, from dra queens to leather boys, is quite sight, however. Open 24 hours day.

LE CIRQUE

58 East 65th Street/ Madison & Park Avenues
☎ 794-9292

The food is so exquisite at this Up per East Side restaurant that yo won't notice the tables being a ta to close and the decor a bit gauch The $29.95 lunch is a feast: thre courses followed by complimen tary coffee, chocolates, and nuts. you want a fine meal in New Yor and can't afford dinner at Boule I'd advise lunch at Le Cirque. Jack ets and ties are required, and res ervations are necessary.

PARIS COMMUNE

411 Bleecker Street

☎ 929-0509

Steamed mussels and roasted garlic chicken (for 2) are some of the many specialties at this gay-friendly restaurant. Reasonably priced. Brunches here, as well as at Tartine (see below), are very popular with the boys.

TARTINE

253 West 11th Street/ West 4th Street

☎ 229-2611

Tartine is one of my favorite restaurants in the Village. They don't take reservations, and they don't serve alcohol, but they will let you bring your own bottle of wine. The food is cheap, elegantly prepared, and delicious. You may have to stand in line if you come for a weekend brunch or dinner, but this is one restaurant that is worth the wait. Save room for three or four of their desserts. *New York Magazine* named their hot chocolate the best in New York City. Credit cards are not accepted.

CAFE SHA SHA

510 Hudson Street, just north of Christopher Street

☎ 242-3021

A cozy place for boys to nuzzle or bump knees while listening to classical music and having a light dinner or cappuccino.

INDIAN

CHUTNEY MARY

40 East 20th Street

☎ 473-8181

Excellent organic Indian food. A perfect find for vegetarians.

DAWAT

210 East 58th Street/ 2nd & 3rd Avenues

☎ 355-7555

Dawat is rated by many as one of the best Indian restaurants in the United States. I don't think I'd go that far. The food at Haveli (see below) is almost as good and much cheaper but Madhur Jaffrey, the famed actress, cookbook author, and restaurateur, serves many excellent and innovative dishes here. It is also very close to the Townhouse Bar and the East Side Club sauna.

HAVELI

100 Second Avenue/ 5th & 6th Streets

☎ 982-0533

I consider this without exception the best and most attractive restaurant on Curry Row. The meals cost a few dollars more than the ones to be had on Sixth Street, but unless you are really counting pennies, try Haveli.

ITALIAN

CAFE DONATELLO

207 Waverly Place/ 7th Avenue & Charles Street
☎ 242-1443
Wonderful coffees, light meals, and desserts are served here, and if you want to sit and talk (or watch the hunks go by) for hours, they won't pressure you, as some busy Manhattan restaurants do, to order more food or leave.

JOHN'S PIZZERIA

278 Bleecker Street/ 6th & 7th Avenues
☎ 243-1680
408 East 64th Street, near 1st Avenue
☎ 935-2895
48 West 65th Street/ Central Park West & Broadway
☎ 721-7001
John's is often said to serve the best pizza in New York. The lines can be long and the service bad, but the prices here are cheap ($8.00 to $13.00 per pie), the ingredients fresh, and the pizza bubbling hot.

TRATORIA SPAGHETTO

228 Bleecker Street/ Carmine Street
☎ 255-6752
Excellent pasta and calamari. Be sure to ask for the free biscotti with your after-dinner espresso or cappuccino.

TWIGS

196 8th Avenue/ 20th Street
☎ 633-6735
Stylish, gayish, Chelsea restaurant. Good food, well priced wines, and a pleasant environment. They bake their pizzas in a wood-burning oven.

ZINNO

126 West 13th Street/ 6th & 7th Avenues
☎ 924-5182
Zinno's is a great place to spend an evening. Situated in a surprisingly large basement of a Village townhouse, the ambiance is wonderfully New York: relaxed yet exciting, bohemian yet sophisticated. The food is also excellent, served in individual portions or family style. There are two sets of jazz each evening, and there is no cover charge. It is possible, but not recommended, to stop in without reservations. The prices are moderate, with entrees between $10.00 and $20.00.

JAPANESE

KIIROIHANA

23 West 56th Street/ 5th & 6th Avenues
☎ 582-7499
Many admirers claim that Kiiroihana serves the best Japanese food in New York. Although prices here are fairly high, the quality of the food and the service is unmatched.

MERIKEN

189 7th Avenue/ 21st Street
☎ 620-9684
Beautiful boys serve excellent sushi and sashimi in an elegant Art Deco setting.

SAPPORO VILLAGE

245 East 10th Street/ 1st Avenue
☎ 260-1330
While Sapporo is not in the same league as Kiiroihana, they serve good food at relatively cheap prices. Their soup is guaranteed to fortify you on a cold winter's day.

MEXICAN

BENNY'S BURRITOS

113 Greenwich Avenue, west of Seventh Avenue
☎ 727-0584
93 Avenue A, South of St. Mark's Place
☎ 254-2054
Benny's serves cheap and delicious San-Francisco-style Mexican food (prepared with white rice and black beans). At the Greenwich Avenue venue, there are too many straight twentysomethings for my taste on Friday and Saturday nights. For a gayer environment, lunch and week night dinners are ideal at this locale. It's always gay on Avenue A.

GABRIELA'S MEXICAN RESTAURANT

685 Amsterdam Avenue/ 93rd Street
☎ 961-0574
Without question, Gabriela serves the best low-mid priced Mexican food in New York. The appetizer platter is excellent, as are the soft tacos, moles, salads, and sandwiches. The food here is authentically Mexican, so try some of the items that you won't find on Tex-Mex menus.

SOUTHERN/SOUL/CARIBBEAN

PINK TEA CUP

42 Grove Street
☎ 807-6755
A little, down-home place where they serve grits, chitlins, and pork chops. The wait for a table can be long.

SYLVIA'S

328 Lennox Avenue/ 126th & 127th Streets
☎ 996-0660
The food served at this Harlem restaurant is good and fairly inexpensive. Sylvia's is also a great locale for brunch after a gospel service or lunch before a walk through the Striver Row district and the Studio Museum of Harlem. Sylvia's is open for breakfast, lunch, and dinner.

TRAMPS

45 West 21st Street/ 5th & 6th Avenues

☎ 463-9400

This moderately priced, New Orleans style restaurant specializes in New Southern cuisine. Very good and very popular.

SPANISH

EL CID

322 West 15th Street/ 8th & 9th Avenues

☎ 929-9332

El Cid serves better Spanish tapas than you can find in most Spanish restaurants. Make reservations if you can.

SRI LANKAN

LAKRUWANA

358 West 44th Street/ 8th & 9th Avenues

☎ 957-4480

If you have yet to try Sri Lankan food, you will discover that it is quite different from Indian cuisine. Lakruwana's specialties include hoppers, pittu, lentil soup, and excellent (coconut milk-based) curries.

THAI

RAIN

100 West 82nd Street/ Columbus Avenue

☎ 501-0776

Rain is definitely the trendiest and arguably the best Thai restaurant in New York. The dining room is huge and beautifully decorated; the food is reasonably priced and excellent, so be prepared for crowds. Reservations suggested on weekends.

REGIONAL THAI TASTE

208 Seventh Avenue/ 22nd Street

☎ 807-9872

Excellent Thai food in gay friendly surroundings.

VEGETARIAN

APPLE RESTAURANT

17 Waverly Place/ Green & Mercer Streets

☎ 473-8888

Good vegetarian fare is served in this airy restaurant situated in the midst of New York University's Greenwich Village campus.

CHUTNEY MARY

(see Indian, above)

QUANTUM LEAP NATURAL FOOD

88 West Third Street/ Sullivan and Thompson Streets
☎ 677-8050
Another good vegetarian find near NYU.

ZEN PALATE RESTAURANT

34 Union Square, near 16th Street
☎ 614-9291
663 9th Avenue/ 46th Street
☎ 582-1669
Zen Palate serves what they call oriental style vegetarian dishes of excellent quality at both their elegantly post-modern Union Square and Theater District locations. Stay away from the mock-meat dishes.

VIEWS, VIEWS, VIEWS

THE HUDSON RIVER CLUB

250 Vesey Street/ 4 World Financial Center
☎ 786-1500
This expensive and elegant restaurant serves foods prepared from ingredients indigenous to the Hudson River Valley. Jackets, ties, and reservations are required. The views of the harbor are beautifully peaceful.

THE RAINBOW ROOM

30 Rockefeller Plaza
☎ 632-5100
The Rainbow Room is set placidly atop what is perhaps the crowning achievement of urban design, 30 Rock. You can have drinks and appetizers in one room, or a full dinner with music and dancing in another. The first is moderately expensive, the second will cost you a good $80.00 per person with dinner, drinks, the music charge, and tip. The atmosphere here is wonderfully romantic, and it is perfectly legal for two men to dance together in this city. Jackets, ties, and reservations are required.

THE RIVER CAFE

One Water Street, Brooklyn
☎ (718) 522-5200
The food here is very good, but what you pay for is the spectacular view to Manhattan.

TAVERN ON THE GREEN

Central Park West/ 67th Street
☎ 873-3200
I'm not too fond of this one, but I'm in the minority. And it is quintessentially New York.

PLEASE KEEP IN MIND:

Unless you are in a large party (usually five or more) your tip will not be included in the bill. It is customary to tip your waiter or waitress 15 percent of your meal's total cost (10% in cheap, low service restaurants and 20% in expensive, high service ones). Tips are not expected at fast food restaurants or cafeterias.

New York City tap water is clean. You may have to ask your wait person for water, but it must be served to you free of charge; that's the law.

Smoking is forbidden in New York City restaurants with more than 30 seats.

As mentioned above, it is advisable, and often imperative, to make a reservation at a fine restaurant such as Cafe Des Artistes or Bouley. Some mid-and-lower priced restaurants take reservations; many do not. If possible, call ahead and ask. Be prepared for long waits at popular restaurants that do not take reservations. Manhattanites are not above waiting in line for an hour and a half to sample anything that's rated the best in town — even pancakes.

Museum restaurants in New York serve uniformly good food. MoMA and the Metropolitan offer two restaurants each, one a moderately priced cafeteria and the other more upscale restaurant with wait persons. The Whitney has an excellent restaurant run by Sarabeth's Kitchen (there are two other Sarabeth's, one at 80th and Amsterdam and one at 92nd and Madison). The Dean and Delucca's at both Guggenheim museums are convenient places to rest and have an espresso or sandwich after touring the galleries.

GLOSSARY

Bagel with a schmear: A bagel with cream cheese.
B.L.T.: A sandwich with bacon, lettuce, and tomatoes.
Check: Your bill for a meal; what you ask for when it comes time to pay.
Coffee, Black: Coffee with neither cream nor sugar.
Coffee, Dark or Light: Coffee with various amounts of milk or cream.
Coffee, Regular: Coffee with either milk or cream, and sugar.
Doggie Bag: At all but the finest restaurants, it is perfectly acceptable to request your waiter or waitress to wrap up any of your leftovers and put them in a doggie bag for you to take with you.
Egg Cream: Made with neither eggs nor cream, this flavored soda-water concoction is a New York tradition. It's made of seltzer, flavored syrup, and milk.
For here or to go?: To eat in or to take away?
Hero: The New York version of a submarine or hoagie sandwich, generally around twelve inches long and six inches in circumference.
Knish: A Jewish food consisting of potatoes and various other ingredients wrapped in dough. Great as a quick snack when you're on the run.
Lox: Salty, smoked salmon, sold in thin slices.
Nova: Nova Scotia Salmon, the same as lox, but with little salt. Perfect with bagels and cream cheese.
Seltzer: Carbonated water, club soda.
Slice: How you order pizza (except where it is sold as a whole pie).
Soda: a flavored, carbonated beverage.
Tab: Either your bar bill or a diet soda.

13: SPORTS, RECREATION & FITNESS

New York has much to offer the sports fan, both spectator and participant. The listings below are exclusively gay only if so specified. Many of the gay sports groups meet at the Lesbian and Gay Community Services Center, 208 West 13th Street (between 7th & 8th Avenues), referred to below as The Center.

BASEBALL/SOFTBALL

NEW YORK METS

Shea Stadium, Flushing, Queens
☎ (718) 507-8499

NEW YORK YANKEES

Yankee Stadium
Bronx, New York
☎ (718) 293-6000
Season: April to October.

BROADWAY SHOW LEAGUE

Hecksher softball fields in Central Park/ West 62nd & 65th Streets, near the Carousel
Celebrating their 42th season in 1996, the Broadway Show League fields about 30 teams from Broadway and off-Broadway shows. Players range from big-name stars to theater ushers. They play three sets of games every Thursday, commencing at 11:30am during an April to August season. Play ends at 5:30pm so everyone can get back to the theater in time for the evening's performance.

BIG APPLE SOFTBALL LEAGUE

Box 475, FDR Station,
New York, NY 10150-0475
☎ 726-1518
A group for gay and lesbian softball enthusiasts.

BASKETBALL

NEW YORK KNICKERBOCKERS (KNICKS)

Madison Square Garden,
7th Avenue/ 31st & 33rd Streets
Hot Line: ☎ 465-5867
Season: October through May.

TEAM NEW YORK BASKETBALL

P.O. Box 2213
New York, NY 10185
☎ 629-2081
Gay basketball team which represents New York at the Gay Games.

BEACHES & SUNBATHING

• For information on the New York beaches see Chapter 14. New Yorkers sunbathe in every city park, open patch, and even on the steps and ledges of public buildings during the summer. Prime spots for gay sunbathers in Manhattan include Sheeps Meadow and the Ramble in **Central Park**; **Riverside Park**; **Carl Schurz Park**; and the pier at the end of Christopher Street.

BICYCLING

• Bicycling in Manhattan's streets can be hazardous and city cyclists foolhardily weave in and out of the zooming traffic. However, it's a safe and very popular sport in **Central Park** where the roads are closed to traffic from 10:00am to 3:00pm and 7:00pm-10:00pm on weekdays and from 7:00pm on Fridays to 6:00am on Mondays. (Holidays: from 8:00pm the night before until 6:00am the next morning.) Also, **Riverside Drive** (on the promenade between 72nd and 110th Streets) and downtown in the **Wall Street** area, which is deserted on weekends. Bicycling to Brooklyn across the **Brooklyn Bridge** is an unforgettable experience (See Chapter 14).

• **Bikes rentals**: at **Central Park** by the Loeb Boathouse near East 74th Street, ☎ 861-4137; **Metro Bicycle** (several locations in Manhattan) call Eastside, ☎ 427-4450; Midtown, ☎ 581-4500; or Westside, ☎ 663-7531 for information on the other stores as well; **Pedal Pusher Bicycle Shop**, 1306 2nd Avenue, ☎ 288-5592.

BILLIARDS/POOL

• Some of the popular billiard halls in the city include:

AMSTERDAM BILLIARD CLUB

344 Amsterdam Avenue/ 76th & 77th Streets
☎ 496-8180

BILLIARD CLUB

220 West 19th Street/ 7th & 8th Avenues
☎ 206-7665

CHELSEA BILLIARDS

54 West 21st Street/ 5th & 6th Avenues
☎ 989-0096

• Many of the Manhattan gay bars have pool tables. You could try **Dugout** and **Stonewall** in the Village; **Rawhide, Eagle's Nest** and **The Spike** in Chelsea and **The Bar, Dick's Bar** and **Tunnel Bar** in the East Village. (See bar listings in Chapter 8)

NEW YORK GAY POOL LEAGUE

P.O. Box 1502, Ansonia Station
New York, NY 10023
☎ 769-8067
The league organizes inter-bar tournaments; proceeds go to AIDS research and charities. Games are played at different bars on different nights of the week (Mon-Thu) from September through May.

BOWLING

BOWLMOR

110 University Place/ 12th & 13th Streets
☎ 255-8188
A 44-lane bowling alley which is open 7 days a week till 1:00am.

LEISURE TIME BOWLING RECREATION CENTER

625 8th Avenue/ at 42nd Street
☎ 268-6909
There are 30 lanes in this venue, situated on the second floor of the Port Authority Bus Terminal, open 7 days a week.

VILLAGE BOWLING LEAGUE

Contact: Gutter George,
310 West 92nd Street, Apt. 4,
New York, NY 10025
☎ 873-0154 or (work) 546-2384
New York's premier gay and lesbian league, goes bowling Wednesdays & Thursdays, Summer and Winter at Bowlmor.

METROPOLITAN COMMUNITY ATHLETIC ASSOCIATION BOWLING LEAGUE

P. O. Box 20604 London Terrace Post Office, New York, NY 10011
☎ 929-6478
A league for gay men and women, which plays at Bowlmor on Tuesdays at 8:30pm.

FOOTBALL

NEW YORK GIANTS

☎ (201) 935-8222

NEW YORK JETS

☎ (201) 935-8500
Both teams play at Giants Stadium, East Rutherford, New Jersey
Season: September-January. Except for a few Jets games, tickets are sold per season and these are difficult to come by. Giants season-tickets are so highly prized that some subscribers bequeath them to their heirs in their wills.

GYMS

• As you know, going to the gym is a major social and cultural activity for many gay men, and New York has its fair share of gym bunnies and muscle queens. There are plenty of gyms in the city, though not all of them offer day memberships. Some gay men prefer not to go to predominantly gay gyms because they are serious about working out and don't want to cruise.

Most of the higher priced hotels have their own fitness facilities. Check at your hotel or with your host for a gym close to you, and refer to gym advertisements the gay press and the *Village Voice*.

The following gyms are exclusively male, gay-friendly environments where even a fancy pubic hair-do won't raise eyebrows!

CHELSEA GYM

267 West 17th Street/ corner of 8th Avenue

☎ 255-1150

Manhattan's best known men-only gym, with free-weights, machines and tanning beds. Day ($10), Week ($25) and One Month ($100) memberships available.

SPA 227

227 East 56th Street/ 2nd & 3rd Avenues

☎ 754-0227

Small but up-to-date, two-level facility catering exclusively to gay men. It offers gym and club facilities, massage therapy, and has dieticians on call. Daily rate for non-members is $20. Remember if working out gets your hormones racing the East Side Sauna is conveniently located in the same building!

MALE/ FEMALE GYMS

AMERICAN FITNESS

120 8th Avenue/ 16th & 17th Streets

☎ 627-0065

This Chelsea gym claims to have the largest free weight space in the city. Day membership costs $15.

BETTER BODIES

22 West 19th Street/ 5th & 6th Avenues

☎ 929-6789

Chelsea's Better Bodies (sometimes referred to as Bitter Beauties!), is a mixed gym with a large gay membership. The day rate is $8.

DAVID BARTON GYM

552 6th Avenue/ at 15th Street

☎ 727-0004

One of the most chic gyms in Manhattan, (known in camp quarters as Dolly Parton's), it is patronized by show-biz luminaries, New York socialites and even porn celebrities. Day memberships are available for $15.

• The YMCA gyms are not officially gay, though you might think so when you look around, particularly at the West Side branch. All the Y's in the city offer full work-out facilities, including swimming pool and sauna. If you are staying at a Y you can use the facilities free of charge. For temporary membership bring your passport/ driver's license to establish your out-of-town status.

YMCA, WEST SIDE

5 West 63rd Street
☎ 787-4400
Weekly ($50) and monthly ($100) memberships are available.

YMCA, McBURNEY

206 West 24th Street
☎ 741-9210
A minimum one-month membership for is available for $75.

YMCA, VANDERBILT BRANCH

224 East 47th Street
☎ 755-2410
Daily ($15) and monthly ($100) memberships are available.

• The New York City Department of Parks and Recreation operates several recreation centers in the city:

The best of these facilities is **ASSER LEVY, East 23rd Street at Asser Levy Place** (one block east of First Avenue), ☎ 447-2020. You can also try the **CARMINE STREET** recreation center, **Clarkson Street and 7th Avenue South** in Greenwich Village, ☎ 242-5228 and the **54th STREET** center, **348 East 54th Street,** ☎ 397-3154. There are no temporary memberships available but a year's membership costs only $25. (You must make payment with a certified check or a money order, available at banks or post offices.) You won't get the same service you will find at private gyms, but Asser Levy is well maintained and newly refurbished, and it has an excellent pool. Members of the city gyms come from all walks of life and represent an interesting cross-section of New York life.

HORSE RIDING

• The only riding stable left in Manhattan is the **CLAREMONT RIDING ACADEMY, 173-177 West 89th Street,** ☎ 724-5100. Private lessons are available. Riders use the bridle path along Central Park's Reservoir, which is a few blocks away from the academy.

OUTDOOR SPORTS

SUNDANCE OUTDOOR ADVENTURE SOCIETY

P.O. Box 2737
New York, NY 10163
☎ 598-4726
A gay and lesbian organization whose members take part in activities such as air sports, backpacking, biking, camping, canoeing, horseback riding, hiking, ice skating, rafting, skiing, and wind surfing. Members are informed about the society's outings through *Crosswinds*, a monthly newsletter.

ROLLERBLADING

• With rollerblades (in-line skates) in vogue, many New York pedestrians are getting on wheels to go about their business on streets of Manhattan. Central Park is the best place to practice your craft.

Rentals:
Peck & Goodie, 917 8th Avenue (54th Street), ☎ 246-6123, with another branch at **1414 2nd Avenue** (73rd Street), ☎ 249-3178. They will also recommend instructors for rollerblading lessons in the park.
Blades Board & Skate, 120 West 72nd Street, ☎ 787-3911, also at 160 East 86th Street, ☎ 966-1644.
Manhattan Sports, 2188 Broadway (at 78th Street), ☎ 580-4753 and 2901 Broadway (at 113th Street) ☎ 749-1454

POWER SKATE

Roller-derby at ROXY
(see Chapter 8)

RUNNING AND JOGGING

• **Central Park** is the most popular spot for Manhattan's joggers. It's quite safe to jog there during daylight hours. The busiest spot is the 1.5 mile track around the park's reservoir which is now named after the late Jackie Onassis (entrances at East and West 90th Streets). There are also runners' lanes designated on the park roads. Other prime jogging areas in Manhattan include: **Riverside Park** (along the Hudson River from 72nd Street to 116th Street); the perimeters of **Gramercy Park** (East of Park Avenue South between 20th and 21st Streets) and **Washington Square** (Greenwich Village).

NEW YORK ROAD RUNNERS CLUB

9 East 89th Street
New York, NY 10128
☎ 860-4455
The club sponsors the New York City Marathon which takes place annually in late October or early November.

FRONT RUNNERS NEW YORK

P.O. Box 87, Ansonia Station
New York, NY 10023
☎ 724-9700
A running and walking club for lesbians, gay men and their supporters, which organizes the annual 2-mile Lesbian and Gay Pride Run every June.

SKATING

• The major rinks in the city include:

ROCKEFELLER CENTER

(lower plaza), 50th Street & 5th Avenue
☎ 757-5731
New York's prime tourist attraction. Open only in the winter.

SKY RINK

Pier 61, Chelsea Piers/ West 23rd and Westside Highway
☎ 336-6100
The city's newest and biggest.

RECREATION WORLD ICE CHALET

World Trade Center
☎ 524-4386

WOLLMAN MEMORIAL RINK

Central Park near 64th Street
☎ 396-1010
A picturesque open-air rink which is crowded on weekends. Open all year round (rollerskating in the summer months).

INTERNATIONAL GAY FIGURE SKATING UNION (IGFSU)

Box 1101, New York, NY 10113
☎ 691-1690; 255-0559
Gay figure skating with same-sex couples and unconventional costuming is now a major Gay Games event. IGFSU has members across America and around the globe.

SOCCER

RAMBLERS SOCCER CLUB

130 Water Street
New York, NY 10005
☎ 344-2936
A gay group which practices in the summer months on Tuesdays and Thursdays from 6:00pm-8:00pm in the Ramble, Central Park (near West 74th Street); Saturdays from 12 noon-3:00pm by the East River (F.D.R. Drive) at East 6th Street.

SWIMMING AND DIVING

• Unfortunately there are not many swimming facilities available to New York visitors. See listings under GYMS for the YMCA, and the New York City Department of Parks and Recreation locations. During the summer months the city recreation centers open their outdoor pools, but you have to put up with hordes of screaming children splashing about.

Some hotels open their swimming and fitness facilities for non-guests. You could try **THE U.N. PLAZA, 1 United Nations Plaza,** ☎ 702-5016 which offers gym, swimming and sauna facilities for $20 per day.

TEAM NEW YORK AQUATICS

Hotline: ☎ 691-3440
A group for gay competition and fitness swimmers, which represents New York at the Gay Games.

VILLAGE DIVE CLUB

P.O. Box 828, Village Station, New York, NY 10014
☎ 769-4487 or (718) 847-1779
A lesbian and gay scuba club.

TENNIS

• The U.S. Tennis Association's Annual US OPEN is held August through September at the U.S.T.A. National Tennis Center, Flushing Meadows-Corona Park, Queens New York, ☎ (718) 271-5100

MANHATTAN PLAZA RACQUET CLUB

450 West 43rd Street/ at 9th Avenue
☎ 594-0554
Five courts, which may be booked by non-members are available.

NEW YORK CITY PARKS DEPARTMENT PUBLIC COURTS

Daily reservation tickets available at CENTRAL PARK COURTS
☎ 280-0206
Open April through October

METROPOLITAN TENNIS GROUP

☎ 802-4768
A gay and lesbian group which meets at The Center.

WRESTLING

• New York's major professional wrestling (and boxing) competitions are staged at Madison Square Garden, 7th Avenue 31st & 33rd Streets, ☎ 465-6000.

KNIGHTS WRESTLING CLUB

P.O. Box 161, Jackson Heights, NY 11372
☎ (718) 639-5141
The club (for both gay men and lesbians) meets at The Center. Men's training: Saturday 2:00pm-5:00pm; Men's wrestling every Sunday at 2:30pm-5:00pm.

METRO GAY WRESTLING ALLIANCE

☎ 563-7066
Meetings on Sundays 2:00pm-5:00pm and Wednesdays 8:00pm-10:45pm at The Center.

14: BEYOND MANHATTAN

by Ben Pesner

THE FOUR OUTER BOROUGHS

If, like most tourists, you spend your entire visit to New York City on the island of Manhattan, you are missing out on four-fifths of the Big Apple — Brooklyn, Queens, the Bronx, and Staten Island. There's no excuse for this behavior. Read on.

BROOKLYN

Visit Brooklyn. Start by walking across Brooklyn's most famous landmark, the stately, romantic **Brooklyn Bridge**. The visual rhythms created by the complex webbing of the bridge's distinctive cablework and the spectacular views of lower Manhattan are, in a word, intoxicating. And there's no better way to appreciate the vitality and beauty of New York's spectacular harbor, except perhaps by reading Walt Whitman's poem "Crossing Brooklyn Ferry".

When the bridge was opened in 1883, it linked two independent cities. Brooklyn had been settled by the Dutch and British in the 17th century. Upon annexing neighboring towns in 1860, Brooklyn became the third largest city in the world. Brooklyn remained independent — with its own newspapers, museums, and transportation system — until 1898, when it joined Manhattan, the Bronx, Staten Island, and the villages and towns that make up the present-day borough of Queens to form Greater New York. Brooklyn has been a special place to multitudes of diverse native-born Americans and immigrants (see the movies *Do the Right Thing, A Tree Grows in Brooklyn*

hoto copyright © Stephen DiMenna

Sophie's Choice, and *Moonstruck*), and more than a few Brooklynites still have not recovered from the departure of the borough's major league baseball team, the beloved Brooklyn Dodgers, to Los Angeles in 1957.

When you reach the Brooklyn side of the bridge, walk down the first stairway to Cadman Plaza, which is the western border of **Brooklyn Heights**. Once a short ferry ride from lower Manhattan, the nation's first suburb is a treasure trove of nineteenth century architecture, graced with many blocks of outstanding brownstone, Federal style, and Greek Revival townhouses. While exploring this neighborhood, which was designated New York City's first historic landmark district in 1965, make your way along Clark, Montague, or Remsen Streets to the famous **Promenade, a** 0.3 mile-long esplanade along a bluff overlooking the upper harbor. Views of the Lower Manhattan skyline are unequalled, especially at twilight. And it's cruisy to boot. The Promenade was built when Heights residents resisted the proposed destruction of the neighborhood to accommodate the Brooklyn-Queens Expressway. The city came up with an alternative plan, and the result is a triple-decker sandwich: two levels of highway hidden under a wide pedestrian walkway. Convenient subways are the 2 and 3 trains at Clark Street and the 2, 3, 4, and 5 trains at Borough Hall, you'll find shops and restaurants on Montague Street.

South of the Heights are the charming neighborhoods of **Cobble Hill** and **Carroll Gardens**, known for their restored carriage houses, historic churches, and Italian bakeries. To the east is **Downtown Brooklyn**, a mecca for bargain hunters, especially along Fulton Street. Further east is **Fort Greene**, home of one of New York's foremost performing arts organizations the **Brooklyn Academy of Music** (see Chapter 10), and beautiful stands of brownstone row houses. This neighborhood is the focus of one of the city's vibrant African-American arts scenes

Visit **Spike's Joint**, film-maker Spike Lee's souvenir emporium, located at No.1 South Elliott Street.

Brooklyn's greatest treasure of urban design is **Prospect Park**, created by the celebrated 19th century landscape artists Olmstead and Vaux (they also laid out Manhattan's Central Park, but they considered Prospect Park their masterpiece). The best way to enter is at **Grand Army Plaza**, a stop on the number 2 and 3 subway lines, and home of the **Soldiers and Sailors Memorial Arch** (you can climb to the top of the arch on Sundays). Follow one of the pleasant but seemingly nondescript pathways into the park, proceeding via an underpass beneath the park's circumferential roadway. When you emerge, surprise! You are at the northern end of **Long Meadow**, a glorious ninety-acre grassy expanse on which to spend a day picnicking, playing frisbee, people-watching, sunbathing, or just doing nothing. Around the meadow you'll find the lake; the Boathouse; the Lefferts Homestead, an 18th century Dutch farmhouse which is now a museum; and the zoo. By the way, the pathways around the zoo and the adjacent wooded area are renowned cruising spots, especially among Black men. Enjoy your day exploring the park, but don't linger past sundown.

Also off Grand Army Plaza is the **Brooklyn Botanical Gardens,** ☎ (718) 622-4433. Though not as large as the New York Botanical Gardens in the Bronx, it's worth a visit, especially in the springtime to catch the cherry blossoms and the spectacular Japanese Garden in full bloom. Take the 2 or 3 subway to the Botanical Gardens station.

The **Brooklyn Museum** and the **Central Library** of the Brooklyn public library system are located on the south side of Eastern Parkway, Olmstead and Vaux's grand boulevard travelling east from Grand Army Plaza through Crown Heights. If the museum, whose collections include over two million objects, were located in any other city, it would be the premiere cultural institution of its region. Sadly, because it is in the shadow of its Manhattan counterparts, the Brooklyn Museum is too often overlooked by out-of-towners and New Yorkers alike.

To the west of Prospect Park is beautiful **Park Slope**, another sumptuous neighborhood of elegant brownstones. Seventh Avenue, the main shopping street, is lined with cafes, bakeries, boutiques, and bookstores; there are plenty of places to have lunch. It's hard not to enjoy a stroll through The Slope, especially since the neighborhood is home to a large, friendly gay and lesbian population.

Other notable Brooklyn neighborhoods include **Williamsburg**, which was an independent city until it joined Brooklyn in 1855. Once the home of Walt Whitman, it is now populated by Italian-Americans, Latinos, and Hasidic Jews. There are also many Hasidim in **Crown Heights**, who live alongside a thriving Afro-Caribbean population including the largest concentration of Haitian-Americans in the U.S. Each September Crown Heights hosts the West Indian American Day Carnival along Eastern Parkway.

Once a swank resort, **Coney Island** and adjacent **Brighton Beach** were made accessible to New York's millions by the construction of the subway system in the early 1900s. Now somewhat seedy, these seaside Brooklyn neighborhoods nonetheless contain the kind of terrific mix that makes New York wonderful. You'll find crowds of people from every walk of life; decaying ruins of once splendid resort buildings; a boardwalk stretching almost three miles along the ocean; and the Cyclone arguably the world's most famous roller coaster, which is the centerpiece of the Astroland amusement park. Get a hot dog with sauerkraut and mustard or sample the deliciously greasy fried seafood at Famous Nathan's (at Stillwell and Sur

Avenues). Or visit the nearby **New York Aquarium,** ☎ (718) 265-3400. The beach and boardwalk are especially pleasant in the cooler months. For dinner, walk along Brighton Beach Avenue through **Little Odessa**, the nation's largest Russian emigre community.

Where the boys are

Brooklyn's lone gay bar is the HOT SPOT at One Front Street, ☎ (718) 852-0139, right under the Brooklyn Bridge. THE SPECTRUM, a gay club at 802 64th Street on the edge of Bay Ridge, ☎ (718) 238-8213, may be lacking in the charm department, but it has historical significance. When you get up to dance you will be grooving on the very same disco floor on which John Travolta churned his pelvis in the 1977 film *Saturday Night Fever*. Brooklyn's cruisy areas include Prospect Park and the Brooklyn Heights Promenade, and the stretch of Shore Road near 95th Street in Bay Ridge.

QUEENS

Most visitors to New York pass through the Borough of Queens one way or another — if only because Queens is the home of both John F. Kennedy and LaGuardia Airports. Until 1898 Queens was a collection of several dozen independent towns and villages; ask a local from whence he hails and he'll name one of Queens's neighborhoods: Jamaica, Maspeth, Flushing, Whitestone, Ozone Park, and so on. The largest of the five boroughs, Queens is one of the most ethnically diverse urban areas in the world, with people from well over one hundred different national backgrounds living here. There are Greeks in Astoria (great restaurants, especially along Broadway), Koreans in Sunnyside, Ecuadorans in Corona, African-Americans in Jamaica and South Ozone Park, Chinese-Americans in Flushing, Irish in Woodside, and on and on. And Jackson Heights has one of the largest gay populations anywhere in New York City.

As for sites of interest, Queens has plenty. Elegant **Forest Hills Gardens** is a quiet enclave of Tudor-style homes and public buildings south of Queens Boulevard at 71st Street/Continental Avenue. If tennis is your sport, check out the West Side Tennis Club, ☎ (718) 268-2300, formerly the home of the U.S. Open. Long before Hollywood became the nucleus of the movie industry, **Astoria** was a film production center. Now the **Kaufman Astoria Studios,** ☎ (718) 392-5600, are back in business again. Woody Allen and Spike Lee often work here. Next door is the **American Museum of the Moving Image** (see Chapter 10). The **Socrates Sculpture Garden** and the **Noguchi Museum in Long Island City** make for an easy trip from Manhattan (see Chapter 10), and provide fine views of the Midtown skyline. **Flushing Meadow/Corona Park** was a once trash-strewn swamp, the desolate "valley of ashes" in F. Scott Fitzgerald's *The Great Gatsby*. Transformed into a park, it was the site of the 1939 and 1964 World's Fairs. This verdant playground is now the home of Shea Stadium, the National Tennis Center, and Queens Theater in the Park. Several buildings from the 1964 Fair are still standing, including what is now the **Queens Museum,** ☎ (718) 529-2905, which houses an astonishing 15,000 square foot scale model of New York City and its buildings. The nearby **New York Hall of Science,** ☎ (718) 669-0005, is worth a visit if that's your scene.

For a different kind of experience, spend a day hiking in the **Jamaica Bay Wildlife Refuge**. The visitors center is located about a mile north of the A train stop at Broad Channel. The refuge, part of Gateway National Recreation Area, is a paradise for bird watchers and anyone else interested in waterfowl salt marshes and the like. Tours are available; call ☎ (718) 318-4340.

Meeting the men of Queens

They don't refer to the place as the Borough of Queens for nothing. Long after midnight, mostly Latino crowds pack KRASH, a popular dance club at 34-48 Steinway Street in Astoria, ☎ (718) 366- 2934 (take the R or G subway to Steinway Street). The gay watering holes in Jackson Heights also attract a predominantly Latino crowd: FRIENDS TAVERN, 78-11 Roosevelt Avenue, ☎ (718) 397-7256; BACHELOR'S TAVERN, 81-12 Roosevelt Avenue, ☎ (718) 458-3131; MAGIC TOUCH, 73-13 37th Road, ☎ (718) 429-8605; and MONTANA SALOON, 40-08 74th St., ☎ (718) 429-9356. If you're in Kew Gardens stop in at HATFIELD'S at 126-10 Queens Boulevard, ☎ (718) 261-8484. The gay bar in Forest Hills is BREADSTIX at 113-24 Queens Boulevard, ☎ (718) 263-0300. For more information, check the listings in *HX* magazine or *Next Magazine*. Cruisy areas: check out the southern edge of heavily wooded Forest Park in Kew Gardens and the late night action in Astoria Park.

THE BRONX

The Bronx — never just Bronx — does not deserve its reputation as an urban nightmare zone. Named after Johannes Bronck, who settled here in 1639, the borough is currently enjoying an upswing in fortune. But although there are plenty of neighborhoods to explore, parts of the borough, especially the South Bronx, are still beset by high crime rates and urban decay.

Not to be missed is the **Bronx Zoo**. Take the number 2

subway to Pelham Parkway or catch a BxM11 express bus operated by Liberty Lines (☎ (212) 652-8400 for bus information). On 264 wooded, rocky acres, it's the largest metropolitan zoo in the country. Favorite exhibits include species from the Himalayas, Jungle World, Reptile Grove, and the spooky bat house where nocturnal species rule the day. For information, ☎ (718) 367-1010. Note: be prepared for your encounter with the most prevalent species in the zoo, present in enormous numbers — human schoolchildren.

Close by is the impressive **New York Botanical Garden**, ☎ (718) 817-8705 (from Manhattan, take the Metro North commuter railroad from Grand Central Station to the Botanical Garden station on the Harlem line). Comprising sixteen different gardens and forty acres of forest, the Botanical Gardens are a horticultural gold mine. There are 2700 plants in the Peggy Rockefeller Rose Garden alone.

Nature enthusiasts should spend a day in **Pelham Bay Park**. Near the last stop on the number 6 subway, the city's largest park contains salt marshes, tidal estuaries, creeks, lagoons, bogs, meadows, islands, and a network of trails by which to explore it all. Close to the park is peaceful **City Island**, which seems more like a sleepy fishing village than a section of the nation's largest metropolitan area.

Other interesting sites

Woodlawn Cemetery (Number 4 subway to the last stop) contains the graves of famous New Yorkers including Herman Melville, George M. Cohan, Joseph Pulitzer, and Duke Ellington. **The Hall of Fame**, ☎ (718) 220-6390, located on the campus of Bronx Community College at University Avenue and West 181st St., houses busts of noted Americans in a rotunda designed by Sanford White. The **Poe Cottage** is an 1816 farmhouse in which Edgar Allan Poe lived from 1846 to 1849, and where he wrote *Annabel Lee* and *The Bells*. The Bronx Historical Society administers the house as a museum; ☎ (718) 881-8900. **Riverdale**, a fancy, countrified community of the North Bronx overlooking the Hudson River, is the home of **Wave Hill**, a 28-acre estate which hosts a variety of performing arts events in the summer.

STATEN ISLAND

A trip on the **Staten Island Ferry** is a terrific way to see the city by water, and at fifty cents for a ride, it's one of New York's greatest bargains. The twenty minute ride (which takes tens of thousands of Staten Islanders to and from work each day) through Upper New York Bay provides spectacular views of the lower Manhattan skyline, Brooklyn Heights, Governor's Island, Ellis Island, and the Statue of Liberty.

Sleepy neighborhoods and hilly terrain give Staten Island an unmistakable suburban quality. Unlike the rest of the city, the populace consistently votes Republican. The best way to explore the borough is by car or bicycle, but most Staten Island sites are accessible by bus from the ferry terminal.

The **Greenbelt** is a 2500 acre nature preserve in the center of the island. Ideal for hiking and bird watching, the wilderness areas include woodlands, wetlands, and open fields noted as a haven for rare wildflowers and migrating birds. ☎ (718) 667-2165 for information.

Richmondtown Restoration, ☎ (718) 351-1611, contains forty preserved sites comprising a fascinating portrait of the community which was the center of island life in Revolutionary War days. At 410 feet above sea level, **Todt Hill** is the highest point along the Atlantic seaboard between Maine and

Florida. **Snug Harbor** at 100 Richmond Terrace is a complex of twenty-eight historic buildings, including several distinguished Greek Revival edifices. Once the nation's first hospital and home for retired sailors, Snug Harbor is now owned by the city. With concerts, art exhibits, and a botanical garden, it is Staten Island's major cultural center. Information: ☎ (718) 448-2500. The serene **Jacques Marchais Center of Tibetan Art**, ☎ (718) 987-4378, is a museum built in the style of a Buddhist temple atop a hill on Lighthouse Avenue.

Locals will tell you that while the center of gay life on Staten Island is St. Mark's Place south of Hyatt Street, a few blocks from the ferry terminal, Staten Island is not a particularly gay-friendly place. Though the borough has a low crime rate in general, two recent vicious gay-bashing incidents have reminded local residents that gay people are still not always safe in their own communities.

BEACHES

When the summer heat and humidity become unbearable, the best way to escape is to go to the beach. There are beaches in all four outer boroughs, and there's plenty of readily accessible sand outside the city borders.

CITY BEACHES

City beaches tend to be noisy, dirty and crowded, but they are easy and cheap to get to. The city's most famous beaches, **Coney Island** and nearby **Brighton Beach**, are worth a visit, but not necessarily for a swim (see Brooklyn above). To get there take the B, D, F, or N trains to West 8th Street or the Stillwell Avenue/Coney Island terminus. The eastern end of Brighton Beach is the cruisiest. The **Rockaway** beaches in Queens are accessible by a long subway ride on the A train, but are probably not worth the trip. You would be better off at the adjacent **Jacob Riis Park**, which is administered by the National Park Service and contains a fine stretch of sand, a large pool and tennis courts. Walk to the eastern end of the beach to meet the mainly Black and Hispanic population of gay men. The Transit Authority runs several buses from various Brooklyn locations; ☎ (718) 330-1234 for details. Crowded **Orchard Beach** in the Bronx was built on landfill in 1936 with sand imported from the Rockaways. It's on Long Island Sound rather than the ocean, so don't go there if you are looking for waves.

OTHER NEARBY BEACHES

If you have a car, check out the surf at New Jersey's **Sandy Hook**, a long spit of sand jutting into the Atlantic from the tip of the Jersey Shore. Drive as far out as you can, park, and keep walking until you come to the gay area. There's also a nude section near Lot G (bring sunblock).

The Long Island seashore contains some of the finest beaches on the East Coast. The best of all is **Jones Beach**, a state park with all the amenities (restaurants, changing rooms, showers) created by Robert Moses in the 1930's to provide a place for New Yorkers to go via automobile to escape the immigrant hordes which had made the city's beaches so crowded. As a result, Jones Beach is difficult to get to by public transportation: take the Long Island Railroad to Freeport (40 minutes) and switch to a bus (20 minutes) for the beach. The fare is $10.50 round trip. For railroad information ☎ (718) 217-LIRR [☎ (718) 217- 5477].

Jones Beach's gay section is an especially popular place to cruise the strand and frolic in the dunes. If you drive, park at Field Six and walk along the beach about a mile or so east. The bus from Freeport drops you off farther west at Field Three, so the walk is longer (allow at least a half hour or forty-five minutes).

A pleasant alternative to Jones Beach is **Long Beach**, which is easier to reach by rail. Once a glamorous Long Island resort town, Long Beach is now a peaceful city of senior citizens and young marrieds, old age homes and luxury condominiums. The beach is wide, clean and relatively quiet. Take the Long Island Railroad from Penn Station (change across the platform at Jamaica); the trip is about 50 minutes and round trip fare is $12 including a beach pass. When you disembark at Long Beach, you are two blocks from the boardwalk. Though there is no one specifically gay section, you'll encounter plenty of other gay people if you keep your eyes open.

Fire Island and the **Hamptons** are probably too far for day trips, but the beaches are exceptional — see below.

SOME PLACES OF INTEREST OUTSIDE NEW YORK CITY

FIRE ISLAND

The undisputed summertime mecca for New York gay men is Fire Island, rivaled only by Key West and Provincetown among the East Coast's hottest gay resorts. This 32-mile barrier island off the Atlantic shore of Long Island contains two gay communities, **Fire Island Pines** ("The Pines") and **Cherry Grove** ("The Grove"). You won't find any cars on the island (they are banned), but you will find sun, sand, surf, and sex in abundant quantities in this hedonistic playground. There's not much to see except the beach and the boys, but hey, who cares. The two villages are separated by a mile-long uninhabited stretch of woods and sand dunes popularly known as the Meat Rack for its around-the-clock erotic activity.

Fire Island attracts a tony crowd — some would say one with attitude. As a general rule, the Pines is more upscale with a concentration of bronzed muscleheads while the Grove draws an older, more ethnically diverse population including many lesbians.

Most people spending time on the island stay in expensive summer house rentals or shares arranged far in advance. There are a few guest houses, but the rooms tend to be tiny — think cabanas. In Cherry Grove try BELVEDERE GUEST HOUSE, ☎ (516) 597-6448; CAROUSEL GUEST HOUSE, ☎ (516) 597-6612; CHERRY GROVE BEACH HOTEL, ☎ (516) 597-6600; and DUNE POINT ☎ (516) 597-6261. In the Pines, try the BOTEL, ☎ (516) 597-6500. Rates are cheaper during the off season (May and October) and on weekdays.

The geography of Fire Island is simple: it's a narrow, east-west stretch of sand with the Atlantic Ocean never more than a few hundred feet to the south. The Great South Bay separates Fire Island from Long Island proper to the north. The Grove is to the west; the Pines is further east. The ferry dock is at the midpoint of each community (on the bay side), and the main wooden walkways run parallel to the ocean with houses arranged off side streets. West of Cherry Grove, the Sunken Forest is a fascinating undeveloped nature preserve. Part of the Fire Island National Seashore, it's well worth a visit. Nude bathers generally concentrate just beyond the eastern end of the Pines. There are three ways to travel from the Pines to the Grove or vice versa. You can walk along the beach, take twisty pathways through the Meat Rack (if you think you can avoid the distractions en route), or hop a water taxi from the ferry slip at $4 plus a $1 tip each way.

Day trips to Fire Island are possible, but complicated. For one thing, there are no public facilities, so finding a place to go to the bathroom can be a challenge. If it looks like rain, stay home. There are no movies, antique shops, or cafes, and most people socialize exclusively with friends at private parties. The island has only a few shops, restaurants, and bars, so there's not much to do except be homosexual (whatever that means). Still, if you want to get out of the city and enjoy the beach and being surrounded by beautiful men in a gay-friendly environment, Fire Island is an experience you shouldn't miss. Who knows, you may make new friends on the beach or on the ferry or in the woods.

Dining on Fire Island: MICHAEL'S on Dock Walk in the Grove is the only inexpensive restaurant on the island. Its indoor/outdoor menu features burgers and other simple fare for breakfast, lunch and dinner. The elegant TOP OF THE BAY restaurant is nearby, ☎ (516) 597-6699; reservations are a must. For dinner or brunch in the Pines there's the Yacht Club, ☎ (516) 597-6010 and the CULTURED ELEPHANT, ☎ (516) 597-6010 on Harbor Walk, and the ISLAND CLUB BISTRO, next to the bar of the same name, ☎ (516) 597-6001. If you need to stock up on provisions, the PINES PANTRY is a convenient grocery store near the ferry dock.

Going out: THE ICE PALACE on Bayview Walk in the Grove is the biggest club on the island. It's part of the Cherry Grove Beach Hotel complex. Happy hour begins at about three in the afternoon, and on weekend evenings dancing continues until dawn. Nearby there's the MONSTRO, which has food, cabaret shows, dancing, and a piano bar. CHERRY'S a friendly bar with a restaurant on the bay. In the Pines, the socially correct follow a rather stringent schedule: the PAVILION, a club near the harbor, is packed for "tea" (i.e. cocktails) from 7:00-9:00pm, only after which does one take dinner. Then it's over to the

ISLAND CLUB (next door to the Pavilion) for "sip and twirl" (drinks and dancing, plus a piano bar) from 11 until 1, and back to the Pavilion for dancing until the wee hours.

Here are some things to keep in mind during your Fire Island visit. Whether you stay for a day or a week, make sure to bring plenty of cash. Everything is expensive, and there are no bank machines on the island. Fire Island is crowded with deer, and along with deer comes Lyme disease, a crippling malady spread by deer ticks. Wear insect repellent at all times. Also, bring plenty of sunblock. And DO NOT walk on the dunes (except along the pathways in the Meat Rack). The sandbars are delicate and prone to erosion, and human interference with the beachgrass ecosystem can be deadly. A hint for day-trippers: you can leave your bag at the coat check at the Ice Palace in Cherry Grove for $3 during late afternoon happy hour.

How to get there: Drive or take the Long Island Railroad to Sayville. The train from Penn Station takes about an hour and a half with a change at either Jamaica or Babylon (for LIRR information ☎ (718) 217-LIRR). Take a taxi or van (Colonial Taxi, ☎ (516) 589-3500; $2 each way) to the ferry slips and a ferry to the community of your choice. For ferry schedules and information ☎ (516) 589-0810. Automobile parking in Sayville is limited and expensive, so arrive early in the day. You may also travel via a luxury bus operated by the Islander's Club, ☎ (212) 255-8014 or ☎ (516) 654-2622.

THE HAMPTONS

The Hamptons are a notorious playground on the East End of Long Island for the wealthy and well-connected. On summer weekends the villages and hamlets which make up the Hamptons are choked with the fabulous and the wannabe fabulous alike. Motels book up early; stay with friends, or make your reservations well in advance. Life slows down considerably from October through May. The gay beach in East Hampton is off Further Lane near Two-Mile Road; South Hampton's gay beach is at Fowler's Lane and Cobb Road. The biggest local gay hangout is CLUB SWAMP & THE ANNEX in Wainscott, which features dining, dancing and piano bar, ☎ (516) 537-3332. The Hamptons are accessible by car or Long Island Railroad. You may also travel via luxury motor coach, or "Jitney" — The Hampton Jitney at ☎ (212) 936-0440 or Hampton Express at ☎ (212) 861-6800.

* * *

Finally, if you are a Friend of Dorothy or if you otherwise revere the memory of **Judy Garland**, you might want to make a day trip north to visit her grave at **Ferncliff Mausoleum**, ☎ (914) 693-4700. Take the Metro North commuter train from Grand Central Station to Hartsdale; complete your journey by taxi. Bring a picnic lunch.

15: ITINERARIES

SO MUCH TO DO, SO LITTLE TIME . . .

Here are a few tips to help you take the best bites of the Big Apple, particularly if this is your first visit to New York. As far as possible focus on one area at a time. I'll help you cover the city by day but I'm sure you won't need my assistance for the nights! (The bars and clubs listed in Chapter 8 will point you in the right direction.) For detailed information on the places mentioned below refer in particular to the preceding Chapters 5 (Sights), 11 (Shopping) and 12 (Eating).

Take the **Circle Line Tour** in the morning (weather permitting). It's a great way to begin your New York experience and will help you get acquainted with the geography of Manhattan. Afterwards, choose from among the many ethnic restaurants on Ninth Avenue in the mid-forties for lunch.

If you find the mid-town towers of Manhattan a bit overwhelming at the beginning, spend your first evening in **Greenwich Village** and its environs. Stroll through the tangled maze of charming streets and visit **Christopher Street**, the traditional gay center of New York. Walk along the riverfront to Battery Park; watch sunset from the piers. After dinner go barhopping in the West Village.

You think the Village is gay? Wait till you see **Chelsea**. Shop at Barney's and A Different Light, dine at any of the tres gay restaurants on 8th Avenue and cruise over a cup of coffee at

The Big Cup. Then check out the trendiest bars in town. If you are spending a Saturday morning in Chelsea, visit the Annex Antiques Fair and Flea Market and then brunch at a popular homo haunt nearby. (Don't forget to check out the Flatiron Building when you are in the neighborhood.)

Midtown Manhattan. After visiting the Empire State Building, begin working through your long shopping lists at Macy's. Times Square, 42nd Street, Grand Central Station, and the Chrysler Building are all within walking distance. If you have tickets to a Broadway show, dine on Restaurant Row or on Ninth Avenue, and then take in the lights of Times Square at night.

Take a stroll along **5th Avenue**. Visit Rockefeller Center, St. Patrick's Cathedral, the Museum of Modern Art, and all the famous stores on The Avenue.

For an alternative New York experience try the **East Village**. Dine at an Indian restaurant on Curry Row or a bistro on Avenue A. Later in the evening check out the funky East Village bar scene — you'll soon find out you're not in Chelsea anymore!

The stockbrokers of Wall Street and the tourists visiting South Street Seaport mingle together in **Downtown Manhattan**. Shop at Century 21, lunch in Chinatown. Take the ferry to Ellis Island and the Statue of Liberty. Or, if you can't be bothered with the crowds, cruise past the monument on the Staten Island Ferry. Walk across the magnificient Brooklyn Bridge and catch sunset over Manhattan from Brooklyn Heights.

You could make a visit to **Central Park** part of a trip to either the Upper West Side or the Upper East Side. If you're on the **Upper West Side**, perhaps for a night at the opera (Lincoln Center), remember to pay a visit to Zabar's, the food shopper's paradise. On the **Upper East Side**, visit the Metropolitan

Museum of Art and any one of the memorable New York art institutions in the vicinity.

Finally, try and find the time to visit **The Cloisters**, the medieval branch of the Metropolitan Museum situated near the northernmost tip of the island — it's one of the most serene spots in Manhattan.

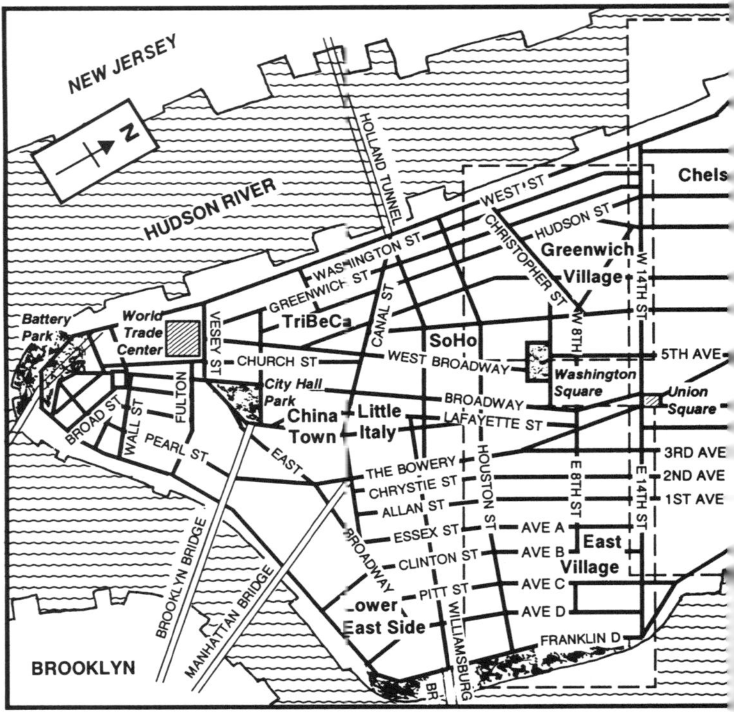
NEW JERSEY
N
HUDSON RIVER
HOLLAND TUNNEL
WEST ST
HUDSON ST
CHRISTOPHER ST
WASHINGTON ST
GREENWICH ST
Greenwich
Village
W 14TH ST
Chels
Battery
Park
World
Trade
Center
VESEY ST
TriBeCa
CANAL ST
W 8TH
SoHo
CHURCH ST
WEST BROADWAY
5TH AVE
Washington
Square
City Hall
Park
BROADWAY
Union
Square
China
Town
Little
Italy
LAFAYETTE ST
BROAD ST
WALL ST
FULTON
PEARL ST
EAST
HOUSTON ST
3RD AVE
THE BOWERY
E 8TH ST
2ND AVE
CHRYSTIE ST
E 14TH ST
1ST AVE
ALLAN ST
ESSEX ST
AVE A
BROADWAY
East
Village
CLINTON ST
AVE B
BROOKLYN BRIDGE
MANHATTAN BRIDGE
PITT ST
AVE C
WILLIAMSBURG
Lower
East Side
AVE D
FRANKLIN D
BROOKLYN
BR

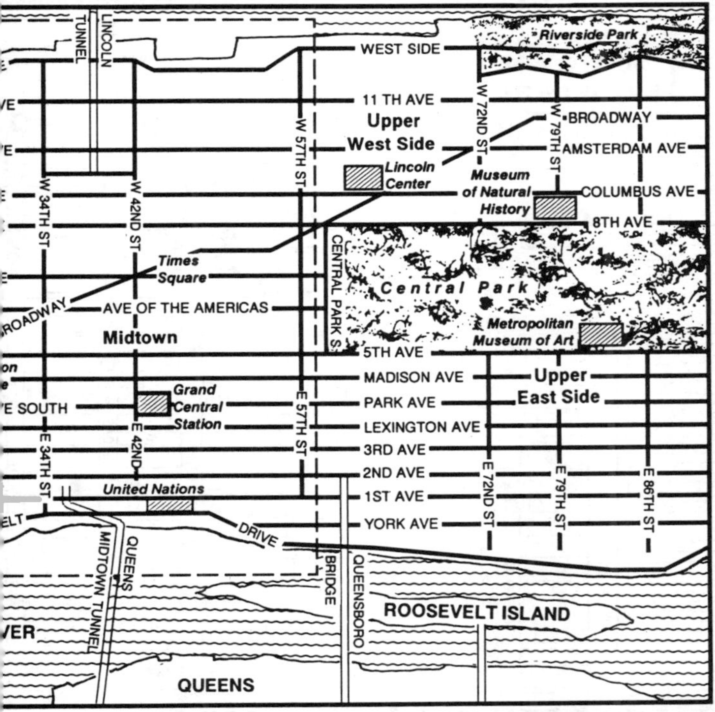
LINCOLN
TUNNEL
WEST SIDE
Riverside Park
11 TH AVE
Upper
West Side
BROADWAY
AMSTERDAM AVE
W 72ND ST
W 79TH ST
W 57TH ST
Lincoln
Center
Museum
of Natural
History
COLUMBUS AVE
8TH AVE
W 34TH ST
W 42ND ST
Times
Square
CENTRAL PARK S.
Central Park
BROADWAY
AVE OF THE AMERICAS
Midtown
Metropolitan
Museum of Art
5TH AVE
MADISON AVE
Upper
East Side
Grand
Central
Station
PARK AVE
LEXINGTON AVE
3RD AVE
2ND AVE
1ST AVE
YORK AVE
E 34TH ST
E 42ND
E 57TH ST
E 72ND ST
E 79TH ST
E 86TH ST
United Nations
DRIVE
MIDTOWN TUNNEL
QUEENS
BRIDGE
QUEENSBORO
ROOSEVELT ISLAND
QUEENS

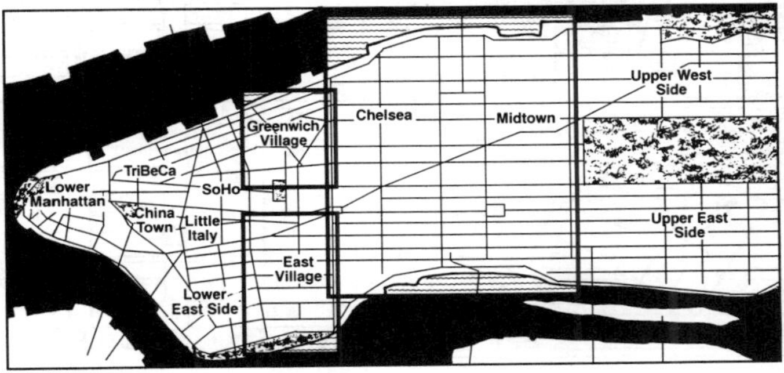
Upper West
Side
Chelsea
Midtown
Greenwich
Village
TriBeCa
Lower
Manhattan
SoHo
China
Town
Little
Italy
Upper East
Side
East
Village
Lower
East Side

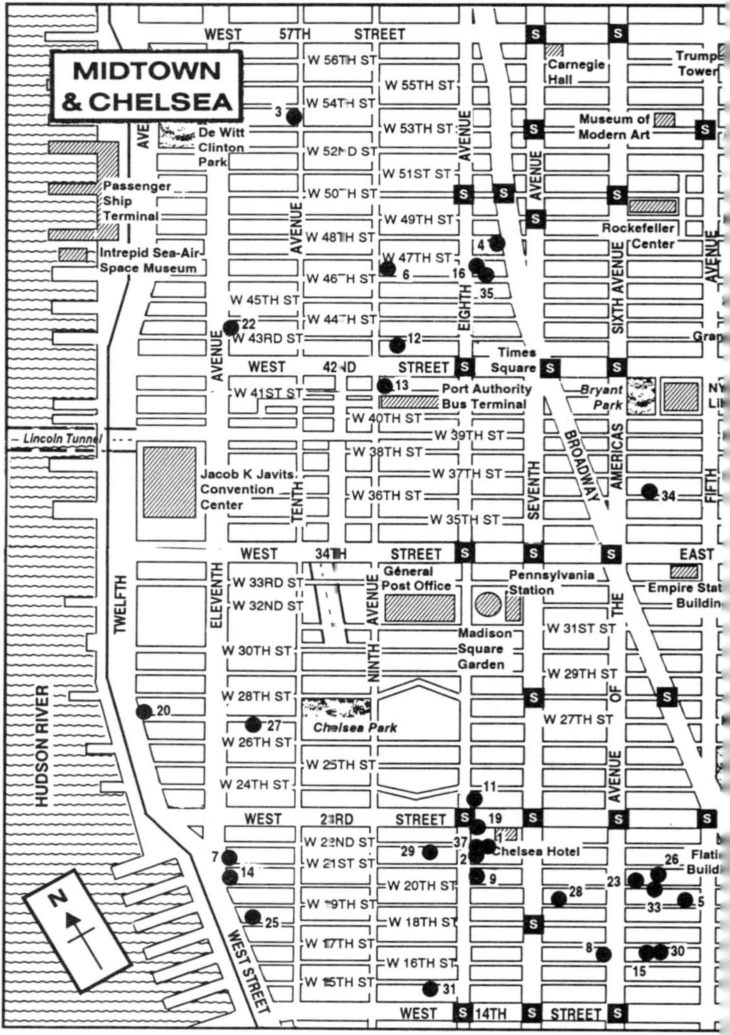

MIDTOWN & CHELSEA
WEST 57TH STREET
W 56TH ST
W 55TH ST
W 54TH ST
W 53TH ST
W 52ND ST
W 51ST ST
W 50TH ST
W 49TH ST
W 48TH ST
W 47TH ST
W 46TH ST
W 45TH ST
W 44TH ST
W 43RD ST
WEST 42ND STREET
W 41ST ST
W 40TH ST
W 39TH ST
W 38TH ST
W 37TH ST
W 36TH ST
W 35TH ST
WEST 34TH STREET
EAST
W 33RD ST
W 32ND ST
W 31ST ST
W 30TH ST
W 29TH ST
W 28TH ST
W 27TH ST
W 26TH ST
W 25TH ST
W 24TH ST
WEST 23RD STREET
W 22ND ST
W 21ST ST
W 20TH ST
W 19TH ST
W 18TH ST
W 17TH ST
W 16TH ST
W 15TH ST
WEST 14TH STREET
Carnegie Hall
Trump Tower
Museum of Modern Art
De Witt Clinton Park
Passenger Ship Terminal
Intrepid Sea-Air Space Museum
Rockefeller Center
Times Square
Port Authority Bus Terminal
Bryant Park
Lincoln Tunnel
Jacob K Javits Convention Center
General Post Office
Pennsylvania Station
Madison Square Garden
Chelsea Park
Chelsea Hotel
HUDSON RIVER
WEST STREET
TWELFTH
ELEVENTH AVENUE
TENTH AVENUE
NINTH AVENUE
EIGHTH AVENUE
SEVENTH AVENUE
BROADWAY
SIXTH AVENUE
AVENUE OF THE AMERICAS
FIFTH AVENUE
N
S
1
2
3
4
5
6
7
8
9
11
12
13
14
15
16
19
20
22
23
25
26
27
28
29
30
31
33
34
35
37

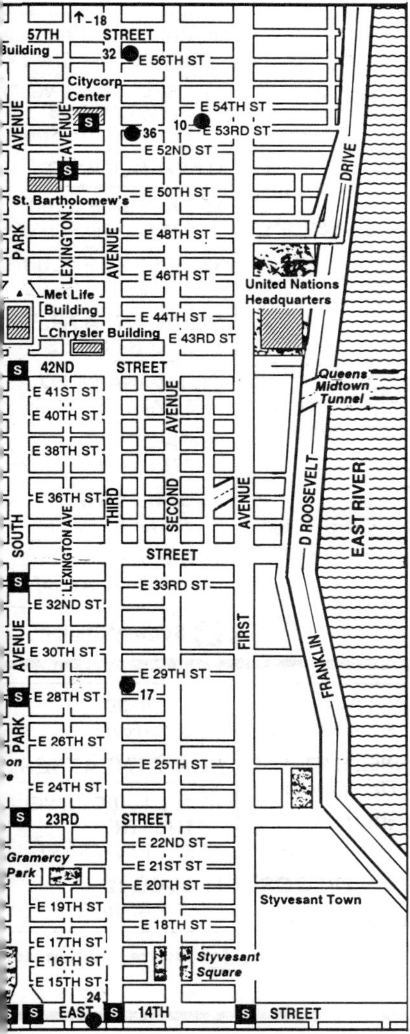

MIDTOWN & CHELSEA

BARS

1 **BARRACUDA**
275 West 22nd Street

2 **THE BREAK**
232 Eighth Avenue

3 **BUSTER'S**
818 Tenth Avenue

4 **CATS BAR**
232 West 48th Street

5 **CHAMPS**
17 West 19th Street

6 **CLEO'S NINTH AVENUE SALOON**
656 Ninth Avenue

7 **THE EAGLE**
142 Eleventh Avenue

8 **KING**
529 Sixth Avenue

9 **RAWHIDE**
212 Eighth Avenue

10 **REGENTS**
317 East 53rd Street

11 **ROME**
290 Eighth Avenue

12 **SALLY'S II**
252 West 43rd Street

13 **THE SAVOY**
335 West 41st Street

14 **SPIKE**
120 Eleventh Avenue

continued over →

MIDTOWN & CHELSEA

15 SPLASH
50 West 17th Street

16 STELLA'S
266 West 47th Street

17 SOUTH DAKOTA
405 Third Avenue

18 TOWN HOUSE
236 East 58th Street

19 TREE HOUSE CLUB
254 West 23rd Street

20 TUNNEL
220 Twelfth Avenue

21 THE WEB
40 East 58th Street

CLUBS

21 EDELWEISS
580 Eleventh Avenue

23 LIMELIGHT
West 20th Street

24 PALLADIUM (BUMP!)
126 East 14th Street

25 ROXY
515 West 18th Street

26 SOUND FACTORY BAR
12 West 21st Street

27 TWILO
530 West 27th Street

GAY BOOKSTORES

28 A DIFFERENT LIGHT
151 West 19th Street

HOTELS

29 COLONIAL HOUSE INN
318 West 22 Street

30 CHELSEA INN
46 West 17th Street

31 CHELSEA MEWS GUEST HOUSE
244 West 15th Street

BATH-HOUSES

32 EAST SIDE CLUB
227 East 56th Street

33 WEST SIDE CLUB
27 West 20th Street

PORN THEATRES/ VIDEO STORES

34 BANANA VIDEO
55 West 38th Street

35 GAIETY
201 West 46th Street

36 LION'S DEN
230 East 53rd Street

37 UNICORN
277c West 22nd Street

S Subway Station

EAST VILLAGE

BARS

1 THE BAR
68 Second Avenue

2 BOILER ROOM
86 East 4th Street

3 CAKE
99 Avenue B

4 CROWBAR
339 East 10th Street

5 DICK'S BAR
192 Second Avenue

6 TUNNEL BAR
116 First Avenue

7 WONDER BAR
505 East 6th Street

CLUBS & DISCOS

8 FLAMINGO EAST
219 Second Avenue

9 PYRAMID
101 Avenue A

PORN THEATRES

10 ALL MALE JEWEL THEATRE
82 East 4th Street

11 BIJOU 82
82 East 4th Street

S Subway Station

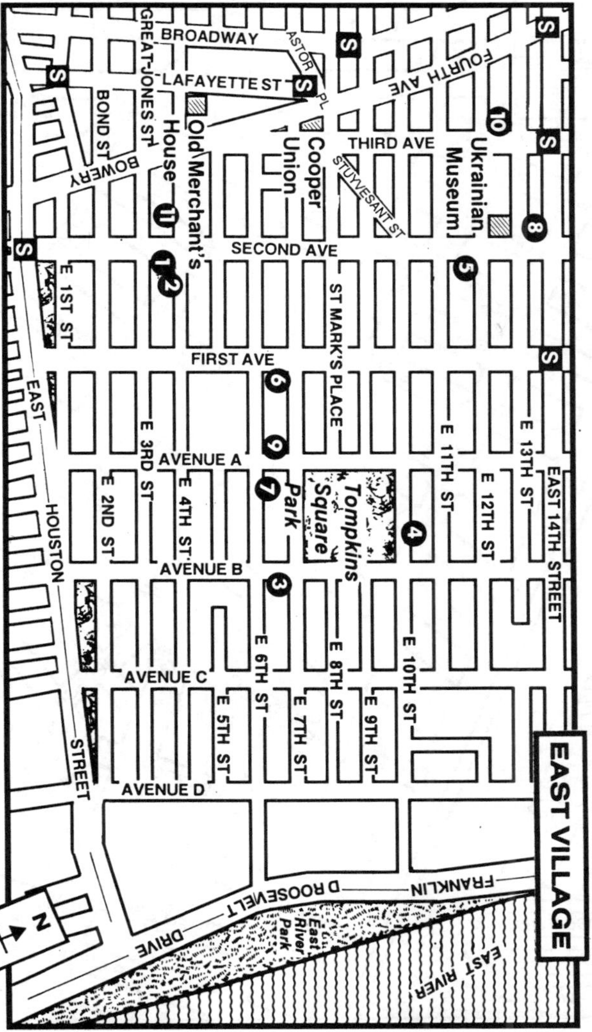
EAST VILLAGE
BROADWAY
ASTOR PL
LAFAYETTE ST
FOURTH AVE
GREAT-JONES ST
BOND ST
BOWERY
Old Merchant's House
Cooper Union
THIRD AVE
STUYVESANT ST
Ukrainian Museum
SECOND AVE
ST MARK'S PLACE
FIRST AVE
AVENUE A
AVENUE B
AVENUE C
AVENUE D
E 1ST ST
E 2ND ST
E 3RD ST
E 4TH ST
E 5TH ST
E 6TH ST
E 7TH ST
E 8TH ST
E 9TH ST
E 10TH ST
E 11TH ST
E 12TH ST
E 13TH ST
EAST 14TH STREET
Tompkins Square Park
EAST HOUSTON STREET
FRANKLIN D ROOSEVELT DRIVE
East River Park
EAST RIVER
N
S
1
2
3
4
5
6
7
8
9
10
11

WEST
14TH
S
NINTH AV
W 13TH ST
LITTLE W 12TH ST
GANSEVOORT ST
HORATIO
JANE
WEST 12TH
STREET
BETHUNE
BANK
WEST
PERRY
CHARLES
WASHINGTON
WEST
GREENWICH
HUDSON
EIGHTH
AVENUE
Abingdon
Square
WEST 4TH
11TH STREET
BLEECKER
10TH STREET
GREENWICH
WAVERLY
SEVENTH
AVENUE
PLACE
Sheridan
Square
GROVE ST
BEDFORD
ST
COMMERCE ST
CHRISTOPHER
BARROW
MORTON
LEROY
CLARKSON
HUDSON RIVER
N

GREENWICH VILLAGE

BARS

1 **BAR d'O**
29 Bedford Street

2 **BOOTS & SADDLE**
76 Christopher Street

3 **DUGOUT**
185 Christopher Street

4 **FIVE OAKS**
49 Grove Street

5 **HANGAR BAR**
115 Christopher Street

6 **JULIUS'**
159 West 10th Street

7 **KELLER'S**
384 West 10th Street

8 **THE LURE**
409 West 13th Street

9 **MARIE'S CRISIS**
59 Grove Street

10 **MIKE'S CLUB CAFE**
400 West 14th Street

11 **THE MONSTER**
80 Grove Street

12 **NUTS & BOLTS LOUNGE**
101 Seventh Avenue

13 **ORBIT**
46 Bedford Street

14 **PIECES**
8 Christopher Street

continued over →

GREENWICH VILLAGE

15 SNEAKERS
392 West Street

16 STONEWALL
53 Christopher Street

17 TWO POTATO
145 Christopher Street

18 TY'S
114 Christopher Street

19 UNCLE CHARLIE'S
56 Greenwich Avenue

20 JACKIE 60
432 West 14th Street

LESBIAN & GAY CENTER

21 THE CENTER
The Lesbian & Gay Community Center, 208 West 13th Street

ACCOMMODATION

22 CHELSEA PINES INN
317 West 14th Street

23 INCENTRA VILLAGE HOUSE
32 Eighth Avenue

GAY BOOKSTORES

24 CREATIVE VISIONS BOOKS
548 Hudson Street

25 OSCAR WILDE MEMORIAL BOOKSHOP
15 Christopher Street

EROTICA & PORN

26 GAY PLEASURES
546 Hudson Street

27 CHRISTOPHER STREET BOOKSHOP
500 Hudson Street

28 HARMONY VIDEO
139 christopher Street

PRIVATE CLUB

29 J'S/ THE HANGOUT
675 Hudson Street

S **Subway Station**